Copyright © 2013 John Harris Sheridan
All rights reserved.

ISBN: 0615891659
ISBN 13: 9780615891651

Acknowledgements

Gary Sotir: The best boss in the TV business (I know because I've been around forever). He's the most honest, knowledgeable and creative guy in television and puts up with a lot. Thanks for putting up with me....

Nacho Garcia: The award winning artist from the El Paso Times the best in the business and my occasional lunch pal and a true friend. He redid the Nickelodeon on the cover of this book.

Claudia Latin, A former Ice Capet: For her research, help and support on this project. In the many years I've known Claudia, I know of no nicer, more reliable or dependable friend.

Henry Seguin, A former Ice Cadet: For all of his help, pictures and great sense of humor as well as years of friendship in Ice Capades, he's my honorary brother.

Judy Davis Kueshner, A journalist from Pittsburgh, for her help with pictures knowledge, friendship and caring as a family friend and neighbor, in Crafton, PA.

Ryan Hall, From KTSM-TV NBC in El Paso, Texas for his photography of the author of this book, many thanks.

Jackie Vera, From KTSM-TV, NBC in El Paso, Texas. My thanks and appreciation for the endless hours she put in, arranging the photographs as well as for her computer expertise.

Jack Bonar, KDBC-TV, CBS in El Paso, Texas. My thanks for always keeping me pointed in the right direction and reminding me to never ask a man if he's from Texas, because if he is, he'll tell you in the first 10 seconds.

Kate Fennell Carlson, KTSM-TV, NBC in El Paso, Texas; for her much needed help on my book and her enthusiasm for the project, to Kate my heartfelt thanks.

Dedicated to:

Thomas J. Sheridan, Brother
John Patrick Sheridan, Son
Kevin Kelly Sheridan, Son
Thomas Brendan Sheridan, Son
and
Maggie Foy, A little Angel friend
who now lives with Jesus.

It Started With
THE NICKELODEON

(The Beginning of the Motion
Picture Theater Industry
and the Family that brought you
Sports & Ice Capades)

BY JOHN HARRIS SHERIDAN

Table of Contents

BUFFALO BILL, CHIEF SITTING BULL & ANNIE OAKLEY	1
THE FAMILY TIME VAUDEVILLE THEATER	7
JEANNE EAGELS IN PITTSBURGH	9
THE PRINCE OF WALES LOVED AMERICAN WOMEN	11
LILLIAN RUSSELL	17
THE AL JOLSON STORY *THE MOVIE*	21
THE EARLY ENTERTAINERS	23
HER NAME WAS "TEXAS GUINAN" AND SHE WAS NOBODY'S SUCKER…	27
THE GREAT MAUDE ADAMS 'PETER PAN'	31
THE BIRTH OF THE NICKELODEON	*33*
THE MOVIE POLICE	39
GUESS WHO CAME TO THE NICKELODEON	41
HARRY WARNER WAS RIGHT	45
LEWIS, MYRON & DAVID O. SELZNICK	47
SAM WARNER MADE THE MOVIES TALK	49
HOWARD HUGHES & "HELLS ANGELS"	51
RICK SEBAK, SANDRA SAGALA & MARY ROBINSON *MY HUNT FOR THE MOVIE "THE LIFE OF BUFFALO BILL"*	53
HARRIS LOVED PITTSBURGH EVEN MORE THAN SHOW BIZ	55
CATHERINE VARIETY SHERIDAN FOUND AND THE VARIETY CLUB IS BORN	59
HARRY HARRIS TAKES A WIFE	63
GENE KELLY & PAT O'BRIEN IN L.A.	65

THE HARRIS AMUSEMENT CO. THE PITTSBURGH HORNETS AND THE DUQUESNE GARDENS	69
PITTSBURGH'S FIRST AND ONLY NBA TEAM	73
JOHN H. HARRIS TAKES A BRIDE	75
THE DUQUESNE GARDENS AND SPORTS	79
PITTSBURGH'S MOST BELOVED HOCKEY TEAM	83
THE START OF ICE CAPADES	87
DONNA ATWOOD AND BOBBY SPECHT JOIN ICE CAPADES	113
HARRIS GOES HIS OWN WAY	125
THE HORNETS 'HIT' MAN	129
THE ICE CAPADES TRAINING CLASS IN PITTSBURGH	131
ICE CAPADES IN ATLANTIC CITY	133
THE BRUCE BARRAGE, IN ATLANTIC CITY	139
ON THE BOARDWALK - IN ATLANTIC CITY	143
THE ICE CAPADES PERFORMERS GROUP AND THE 'KIDS'	145
ICE CAPADES - ON THE ROAD	147
ICE CAPADES AND THE TOAST OF THE TOWN	157
THE GREAT HUNTING CAPER	159
THE LAMBRETTA RACE	161
THE "FINE" PARTY	167
THE GREAT CROCODILE CAPER	171
THE ICE CAPADES IN LOS ANGELES	175
HANS BRINKER AND THE SILVER SKATES	181
ICE CAPADES AND THE UNION	193
THE KLUGE ERA	197
THE AUDIENCES STARTED TO DECLINE	199
ADDITIONAL NAMES AND DATES	205

BUFFALO BILL, CHIEF SITTING BULL & ANNIE OAKLEY

Sometime around 1885 word reached John P. Harris that Buffalo Bill's Rodeo may no longer be coming to Pittsburgh; so, Harris decided to go to Buffalo, NY and try to talk Buffalo Bill into coming to Pittsburgh and allowing Harris and his brother-in-law Harry Davis to produce the rodeo. I never learned how those talks turned out; but, I do know it never happened. Harris never produced the rodeo.

While in Buffalo, NY Harris not only met Buffalo Bill; but, the remarkable sharpshooter Annie Oakley as well as the great Chief of the Lakota Sioux, Sitting Bull. The Chief was only with the rodeo a short time, for about four months. Some said it's because he didn't like traveling around the country and others say that because the minute he entered the rodeo arena the audience booed until he left. I can only surmise it was because he, along with Chief Gull and Chief Crazy Horse defeated and killed General George Custer at the Battle of Little Big Horn, in 1876. The audience reaction to the Chief was not very pleasing to him for one reason or another so he decided to leave the rodeo and return home, where he continued his resistance against the United States Army. Chief Sitting Bull was killed in an altercation with the BIA Police (Bureau of Indian Affairs), in 1890. Today Chief Sitting Bull is buried at Fort Yates, North Dakota. He is remembered by many as a Holy Man and the most important and greatest Chief of the Lakota Sioux Nation. Harris always thought of the Chief as a man who lived by his word and always kept that word. If you want to know more about Buffalo Bill and Chief Sitting Bull, I would suggest you read Author Sandra K. Sagala book. She is the most learned person, I've ever talked to relative to Buffalo Bill. Sandra K. Sagala is the author of the book "Buffalo Bill on the Silver Screen" and available through University of Oklahoma Press, fall 2013.

Years later Harris told his daughter Mary there was little interest from Chief Sitting Bull about doing a movie, for some reason he didn't trust movies. Movies weren't real big in 1885 and even though the Chief didn't trust them Buffalo Bill was opened to the idea until the Chief was killed, in 1890. They never mentioned it again until 1909 and in 1910 it became a reality. Harris ended up producing "The Life of Buffalo Bill" that was more than a hundred years ago, starring, William Fredrick "Buffalo Bill" Cody. Buffalo Bill wasn't Harris' first movie experience. In 1908 he produced a motion picture called "The Great Train Robbery" with a cast of children, in McKeesport, PA. Harris contacted Edwin S . Porter a director and cinematographer. Porter was the original cinematographer on the 1903 motion picture of the same name. The motion picture met with a good amount of success.

Buffalo Bill and some of the Lakota Sioux Indians that were in his rodeo.

Buffalo Bill, Taken in El Paso, Texas in the late 1800's.

Annie Oakley.

THE FAMILY TIME VAUDEVILLE THEATER

It was June, a warm and humid day, on Diamond Street in Pittsburgh in the late1880's and the fans were churning at full blast in the Vaudeville Theaters and in 'The Family Time Vaudeville' and 'The Avenue Vaudeville Theater' things were no different; but, this was to be expected this time of the year in Pittsburgh, there would be no air conditioning for another fifty years or so, fans were the air conditioning of the day. The Avenue Vaudeville Theater, is still at the same location; but, now it's called The Warner and they no longer offer Vaudeville, which is probably unfortunate because there are so few places for young entertainers to work and learn their craft.

Vaudeville consisted of mixed specialty acts such as musicians, dancers, singers, comics, acrobats, and magicians. The performers would bring their own accompanists or just use the theater's piano/organ player. However, The Avenue Vaudeville Theater and The Family Time Vaudeville offered something different. Between acts, Harris would drop down a muslin curtain and play a three to five minute movie, from a hand cranked projector which he got from his friend Thomas A. Edison, in New Jersey. These would be clips of a rose opening in slow motion, a horse jumping off a cliff in Mexico, dancers in slow motion and divers jumping off a high diving board etc. This was the beginning of something that was about to change the theater business, as the world knew it….It was actually the beginning of The Motion Picture Theater Industry. Even Thomas Edison told Harris "The long movie thing you keep talking about is just a germ of an idea; but, it's an idea." Harris and his father John A. Harris also ran the Harris Comedy and Specialty Company in 1897, showing Pittsburgh's first motion pictures, between acts. The motion pictures ran between 3 minutes and 5 minutes. So, Harris felt he knew what the public wanted. He was positive people would sit for an hour or so the watch a motion picture……..And as it turned out, he was right !!!

JEANNE EAGELS IN PITTSBURGH

JOHN P. HARRIS AND HIS partner and brother-in-law Harry Davis were getting ready for one of the big acts of the day, most popular anyway, her name was Jeanne Eagels. Jeanne was a little girl, with more talent and personality than any other 14 year old. She changed the spelling of her last name, from Eagles to Eagels because she thought it looked better on the marquee and to the public, who was going to argue with her? Jeanne could sing like an angel and dance like the great Anna Pavlova (well almost) and she was just 14. Those who watched her through her career said she was truly a phenomenal actress.

John P. Harris was concerned about Jeanne's safety; So he had 'Big Ted West' the Irish usher/bouncer watch her closely, to make sure she wasn't bothered by the public or even by the other acts. Even at 14 she was just beautiful and an exceptional actress, doing Hamlet and other Shakespeare plays in a traveling stock company. She was a real talent. That's what my Mother told me, her father (J.P. Harris) told her. I wasn't born in those days, but heard about her from my Mother, Aunts and Uncles as well as old friends of the family. In Vaudeville, Jeanne as well as the other performers, did 4 shows a day, six days a week, with her Mother standing in the wing and Ted West in the other wing, watching it all. On Sundays, Pennsylvania had the blue law, which meant almost everything was closed on Sunday; so, Jeanne and her Mother would accompany Harris to the family home for dinner with his family and a swim in the family pool, in Crafton, a suburb of Pittsburgh. In the early 19 hundreds there were very few private pools in Pittsburgh. So, it was a real treat to take a swim in the private pool, especially in Pittsburgh. That was to be Jeanne's first and last year in Pittsburgh. She and her Mother never returned.

However, because Jeanne was such a beautiful and talented young woman I though we should take a quick look at her career. A short time after Vaudeville, Jeanne was appearing in the Ziegfeld Follies and was discovered by Producer David Blasco. David offered her the starring role in his new Broadway show. "Daddies" and a lot more!!! she took the FIRST part of the offer and became the hottest thing on Broadway. However, Jeanne walked out on the hit play, didn't even look back. becoming the first major star ever to walk out, on an established Broadway hit. And she did it because Blasco wouldn't let her alone, he was there every night and at every rehearsal hounding her and she just couldn't take it anymore….. Today it would be labeled sexual harassment…..So, she quit, walked out, said adios !!!

THE PRINCE OF WALES LOVED AMERICAN WOMEN

JEANNE WAS SO BEAUTIFUL SHE had the same problem all of her short life. It happened with the famous theater owner Lee Shubert of the Shubert Theater and believe it or not, it happened with His Royal Highness The Prince of Wales, who repeatedly asked her to marry him. As the Prince of Wales he was the future King of England. And wouldn't you know he later became King…..King Edward V11l.

The Prince of Wales (King Edward VIII) loved American women and nothing stopped the Prince from looking for his American girl, which ultimately forced him to abdicate his position as King, and marry as he called her, "The Woman I Love." The King made one of the most moving speeches about the woman he loved, saying at the time of his abdicating: "I have found it impossible to carry on the heavy burden of responsibility and to discharge my duties as King as I wish to do, without the help and support of the woman I love." So Edward abdicated to marry the woman he loved. Her name was Bessie Wallis Warfield, then Spencer, then Simpson. The King abdicated the throne and was made Duke of Windsor, by his brother George VI and married his American girl. The King knew that he would have to abdicate, because Parliament would never permit a Monarch to marry a woman, whose husband was still alive and Bessie had two of them, both alive and she was an American and a commoner at that, which was also a problem for Parliament and the English people at that time. On top of that, as King, he was the head of the Church of England….. That's kind of like the Pope hooking up with Lady Ga Ga. Edward VIII was replaced on the throne by his brother George VI, father of Queen Elizabeth ll and the subject of the Oscar® winning motion picture, "The King's Speech." I guess it would be fare to say had Jeanne married the Prince of Wales, she would have become the Duchess of Windsor. It's funny how things turn out.

However, it was not to be. Jeanne Eagels ultimately acclaimed by many as the greatest actress of the 20th century died October 3rd 1929 at the age of 39, in New York City of what her friends said were mysterious circumstances; but, the coroner said she died of an overdose of heron.

Few know it; but, the Royal Family came from German stock and for years the people of the British Empire and even the United States was concerned with the British Royal Family and their love affair with the Germans. Hitler was always admired by King Edward VIII, later the Duke of Windsor and so the Duke accompanied his wife the Duchess of Windsor on a visit to Germany as guests of Adolf Hitler, in 1937. Many of the British people liked the harsh way the Nazi Government dealt with the Communists, throwing many into prison camps like Auschwitz-Birkenau and killing others. It's been said that should Germany defeat England in World War II, Hitler would have looked at the Duke of Winsor as a possible head of state of a subjugated Britain.

In 1917 during World War I, The Royal Family thought it prudent to change their German name from Saxe-Coburg- Gotha of the House of Wettin to Windsor, their present name, concealing their German linage to many. As recent as the 1980's Princess Michael of Kent's father Baron Gunter von Ruibnitz was exposed as a former Nazi and SS Officer. Queen Elizabeth's husband Prince Philip had a sister who was married to Christopher of Hess-Cassel, an Army Colonel and an SS-Standartenfuhrer (Colonel). All four of Prince Phillips sister's married high ranking German officers. I don't know why we didn't know about it then……well maybe I do !!!

However, when Jeanne Eagels was still in Vaudeville she appeared with the greatest of Vaudeville stars, and was loved by all of her co-performers and especially the public. Harris made sure she worked with people who wouldn't bother her, like comic Luke Barnett, the great clown Joe Jackson or even singer Al Jolson and his brother Harry, who worked with him in the early days.. Harris knew the young Al Jolson and how much he liked the ladies so they had an understanding. As it was, Jolson was only a few years older than Jeanne; but he had the street smarts she lacked. It was also before he started wearing black-face, that he learned from Charlie Case a Vaudeville singer and Jolson wore it throughout his career. But, he had that certain something that would make him a star and Harris recognized it.

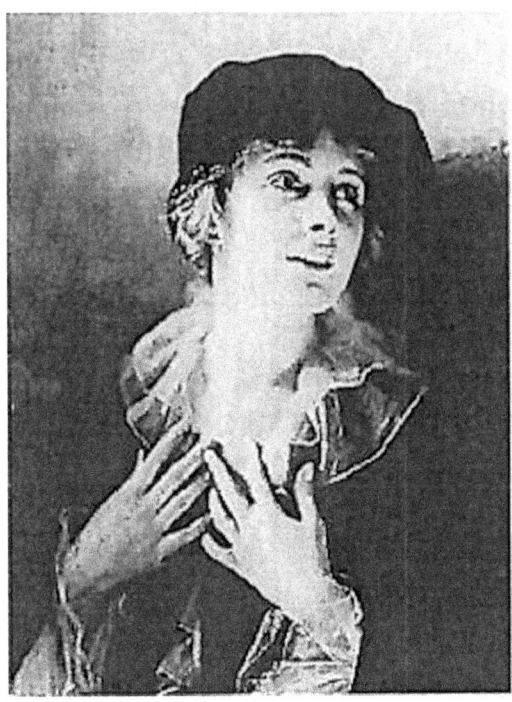

Jean Eagels

Vaudeville Theater, similat to those in Pittsburgh in the late 1800's

Joe Jackson, Vaudeville/Ice Capades.

LILLIAN RUSSELL

SOMETIME JEANNE EAGELS WORKED WITH Lillian Russell. Lillian was married to Alexander Moore, the publisher of the Pittsburgh Leader Newspaper, The largest newspaper in Pennsylvania. Russell lived in Pittsburgh and she was available most of the time, to fill in at the theater if someone was sick or hurt. Even though she was married, Lillian had a very wealthy and flamboyant boy friend in New York City named James "Diamond Jim" Brady, who hung around with people like the Vanderbilts, The Woolworths and even the producer Florenz Ziegfeld. "Diamond Jim" was always giving Lillian gifts. He bought Lillian her own luxury railroad car, so she could travel to New York to see him, the most elegant way to travel in those days.. All she had to do, was hook her railroad car to a train going to New York like the New York Central Railroad or the P&LE (The Pennsylvania and Lake Erie) or the B&O (Baltimore & Ohio). Diamond Jim even bought her a gold plated bicycle as well. He also bought one for himself so, he and Lillian could pedal around Central Park together. can you imagine them doing that today, I don't think it would play well today with the Homies, in Central Park. Lillian was a high maintenance girl and performer. she was not well liked by those with whom she Worked, especially John P. Harris and Harry Davis. Lillian once walked into John P's office as he was doing some paper work and he just looked up and asked how he could help her. Lillian responded, "A gentleman always stands when a lady enters the room" John P, who knew about her tryst with Diamond Jim and the weight lifter said, "I always stand when a LADY enters the room".

Lillian was running around with Diamond Jim as well as strong man "The Great Sandow" and Lillian had a husband, that everybody liked at the same time, which alienated a lot of people. However, with all of her 'life-experience', she wrote a column in her husband's newspaper instructing women how to act like ladies. That's like John Gotti teaching Hoover how to run the FBI. When asked to comment on her newspaper column Harris replied, "Sometimes to be silent is to be most eloquent".

Lillian would give the women of Pittsburgh, Western Pennsylvania and surrounding areas advice on "How to Sit and Walk and the Benefits of Vigorous Dancing". Lillian wrote, "Some women who are in business assume a manner of stiffness in their walk and carriage which is unwomanly "Russell wrote, "Such women should dance......they should lighten up, when away from business drop responsibilities and feminize themselves."....... Now, there is a little tip for you 'working girls' !!!

Thanks to Len Barcousky of the Pittsburgh Post-Gazette, for his research and advice. One other thing about Lillian if you're up to it! When Alexander Graham Bell initiated long distance telephone service May 8, 1890, It was Lillian Russell's voice that was first heard singing "Sabre Song".

Lillian Russell in "The Brigands"

Lillian Russell

THE AL JOLSON STORY

The Movie

A FUNNY STORY ABOUT, "THE WORLDS Greatest Entertainer", that's what they called Al Jolson. Actor Larry Parks starred in the movie "The Al Jolson Story" playing Jolson. So, when the studio decided to do a spin off in 1949 called, "Jolson Sings Again". Al decided to take a screen test, for the opportunity to play himself. Now, would you call that type casting or what? Well, anyway guess what!!! He failed his own screen test and didn't get the part to play himself. It went to Larry Parks again, the actor that did the first movie, "The Al Jolson Story".

Shortly afterwards Larry Parks had great problems with his career, when it was learned that he was a member of the Communist Party. His career went down hill and he found jobs were almost impossible to get.

Even though Al Jolson didn't get to play himself, he was still the biggest thing in show business, bigger than Frank Sinatra, Perry Como or even Bing Crosby, when they were at their peak in the 40's. Jolson was the first singer to sell 10 million records.

Al Jolson

THE EARLY ENTERTAINERS

These were the people who entertained the public, in The Harris and Davis Vaudeville Theaters, in Pittsburgh during the late 1800's. Some of the performers were very high maintenance like Lillian Russell. Others, like Maude Adams, Joe Jackson, Al Jolson and Luke Barnett went out of their way to be helpful, but Barnett was a real gentleman with a great personality, not what you would expect from his loud mouth stage persona. That's what my Grandfather told my mother. I never met my Grand Dad; but, I met Barnett. My Grand Father died 12 years before I was born; but, I almost feel like I know him.

This was a great time to be alive. It was a great time for the creative, entertainment and music world. The great Nijinsky, known the world over as Vaslav Nijinsky the greatest ballet dancer who ever lived was dancing, choreographing ballets and Broadway type shows. Maurice Ravel, the composer of "Bolero" originally called "Fandango", was working on "Jeux d'eau" and the score of "Carmen" and still writing music. His friend Igor Stravinsky was still conducting the worlds great orchestra's as well as composing very original and controversial music such as "The Rite of

Spring." and George Gershwin was just a young piano player, in New York in those days, not yet known to the public. He was playing the piano, for song peddlers, his "Rhapsody in Blue" had yet to be written. Pablo Picasso the cubist painter was painting in France and changing the art world. However, the war to end all wars, (I've got to repeat that one: The War to end All Wars), was just around the corner, World War l. My father Andrew Sheridan served in that war and my family was very proud of him, he lied about his age and joined the Army at 16. You could do it in those days, because computers were yet to come on the scene. He was sent to France, to fight the Germans, became a sergeant in combat and was shot by the Germans receiving a Purple Heart, all before he was seventeen, even with the rank of sergeant and a Purple Heart he was still too young to serve. Andrew Edward Sheridan returned to Pittsburgh, becoming a high school teacher at Crafton High School in Pittsburgh and later a lawyer, graduating from Duquesne University. Sheridan practiced law in Pittsburgh and Western Pennsylvania....

Andrew E. Sheridan, age 17, Sergeant, US Army 1917, My Father.

HER NAME WAS "TEXAS GUINAN" AND SHE WAS NOBODY'S SUCKER..................

T HERE WAS ONE ACT IN Vaudeville that used to give both Harris and Davis apoplexy just about every time she walked out on stage, she would shout out to the audience, "Hello Suckers" Harris just cringed whenever he herd her say it. She was a Texan named Texas Guinan. Harris and Davis hated calling the theater patrons 'Suckers' because they thought she was talking down to the audience, but the people loved it and she wouldn't consider changing it. So, "Hello Suckers" stayed in. As a matter of fact Harris and Davis started to see the levity in it and began calling each other "Sucker" when nobody was around. Both Harris and Davis thought the world of Texas Guinan, as did everyone she came in contact with

They said her heart was as big as Vaudeville it self. She was born Mary Louise Cecilia Guinan known as Texas Guinan, from Waco, Texas. She was an actress in silent movies as well as a performer in Vaudeville. Later on she became known as, "The Queen of the Night Clubs" operating them during probation in defiance of the law. But she was a friend of

Mayor James J. "Jimmy" Walker, a former lyricist and later one of the most famous, popular and powerful Mayors of New York. The Mayor had big time mob ties, which I'm sure had something to do with Miss Texas staying open. At about the same time the powerful Irish mobster Owney Madden owned, the famous "Cotton Club" and eight other clubs and because of his friendship with Mayor Jimmy, he sold liquor right through the 18th amendment. In those days, the only way to stay in business, was to get your 'Booze' from organized crime and to pay off certain city officials and I'm sure Mayor Jimmy facilitated all of that.... Mary Louise Cecilia "Texas" Guinan was born in 1884 in Waco, Texas and died in 1933 at the age of 49 in Vancouver, B.C. Canada. The Great Bandleader Paul Whiteman was one of her Pallbearers. Seventy five hundred mourners attended her funeral including many of the 'A' list stars of the day.

'Maria Louise Cecilia "Texas" Guinan.(1884-1933)

There were great Vaudeville entertainers to play Pittsburgh in the eighteen and early nineteen hundreds and other than Jeanne Eagels an obvious Harris favorite and Texas Guanin, Al Jolson, Luke Barnett and the Barrymores, Ethel and Lionel, Sarah Bernhardt, Maude Adams, Eddie Foy, George M. Cohan and magicians, Howard 'The Great' Thurston and Harry Houdini as well as the greatest clown of them all Joe Jackson Jr. who later worked for John P's son John H. Harris in Ice Capades. I saw him in the ice show in the late 40's, when I was only five and I still remember his act, old black torn clothes, a black bowler hat, a big red flower in his lapel and a bicycle. That's all it took to bring the house down and he did it every night.

'Joe Jackson Jr., Vaudeville & Ice Capades'

Later Harris and Davis opened the Schenley Players Theater, a very small but a beautiful and intimate theater, a stones throw from the University of Pittsburgh, on Forbes Street. This theater was designed for nothing; but, the highest form of entertainment and featured Roxanne Lansing, George Alison and the greatest Russian ballerina ever Anna Pavlova.

'THE GREAT MAUDE ADAMS 'PETER PAN'

BUT ONE OTHER ENTERTAINER STANDS out she was a young Mormon girl named Maud Adams. She was born in Salt Lake City to wealthy parents. However, in spite of that, she became the highest paid actress on Broadway making more than 1 million dollars a year, in 1905 money, a tremendous sum. Sir James M. Berry, the Knighted Englishman and author of "Peter Pan" was so impressed with Maud he choose her to play the very first "Peter Pan". Maude Adams played Peter Pan on Broadway and was an instant success.

Maud was a very sensitive person and fortunately, because of her wealth, if Maud thought an actor or actress was being under paid for his/her work, she would quietly subsidies their pay, with her own money, I can't imagine that happening today; but, it did then and included stage hands as well as cast members. Maud was loved by everyone who ever worked with her and most of those who watched her perform on stage. All but one: Willa Cather a writer and drama critic for The Pittsburgh Home Monthly. Willa referred to Maud Adams as being "unattractive, with a nasal twang voice, unpardonable" Willa had her targets too and she wore them everyday. To her mother's chagrin, at a young age, Willa cut he hair like a man's and wore pants. Not the thing to do in the late 1800's; But; today, she would probably get a TV Show out of it. Willa was an accomplished writer winning a Pulitzer Prize for "One of Our Own".

Even though Maud Adams was a Mormon and a devoted one, she loved the Catholic Church very much, maybe it was the pageantry, the tradition or the nuns and priests ; but, whatever it was Maud loved it. She donated a home to the Church in Lake Ronkon, NY. She was always very generous to the clergy. When Maud Adams passed away in 1953 she was buried in the cemetery of the Sisters of the Cenacle, in Lake Ronkon, New York. I'll bet there were nuns and others saying: "Saints Preserve Us" or was it "Latter Day Saints Preserve Us?"

But, Maud Adams will always be remembered as the very first Peter Pan, followed by Mary Martin and Donna Atwood.

THE BIRTH OF
THE NICKELODEON

The Beginning of the Motion Picture Theater Industry

JOHN P. HARRIS WAS CONVINCED that the motion picture business could stand on its own, without singers, dancers and comedians, in the Vaudeville theater. So, he decided to open the world's first all motion picture theater, no more three to five minute clips, no vaudeville performers, only motion pictures. Harris talked to his brother-in-law Harry Davis about finding a place for the theater and it just so happened that Harry had a place at 433-435 (now 441) Smithfield Street, in downtown Pittsburgh, across the street from the old Kaufman's Department Store. Harry was more interested in legit theater and the Vaudeville aspect of the business; but, since Harry had the building they became partners in this new venture.

NOTE: I feel I have to point this out now, because it recently has come to light. John P. Harris opened the Nickelodeon June 19, 1905. It was considered the first all motion picture theater in the world, meaning it was a theater that played only movies and movies exclusively not interspersed with Vaudeville acts. The Harris-Davis Nickelodeon was recognized as the first all motion picture theater in the world by the newspapers, Hollywood Studios as well as the Commonwealth of Pennsylvania, who honored it with a Brass Plaque on the side of a building where the Nickelodeon once stood.. For 100 years plus it was the universal belief that The Nickelodeon was the first all motion picture theater, in the world.

Now, there are a few people popping out of the woodwork who claim they were showing motion pictures exclusively, before 1905. Well, I doubt it or we would have heard about it sometime in the last one hundred plus years; but, we didn't….. If they were showing motion pictures at all, I'm sure they were being shown along with Vaudeville acts and they were of the three to five minute shorts variety. It wasn't until after 1905, after the Nickelodeon opened that there was a sudden explosion of little theaters around the country; but, not until after 1905. The Warner Brothers and their Cascade Theater, in New Castle, Pennsylvania in 1907, built with Harris' help. There was Louie B. Mayer (of the famed Metro-Goldwyn Mayer Studios) Mayer had the Globe Theater later, The Orpheum, in Haverhill, Massachusetts also built in 1907 and during that time more than three thousand Nickelodeon type theaters were built.

Harris started working on his theater right away. he was a friend of Thomas Edison and visited him in New Jersey frequently for advice.

Edison actually had the first motion picture production company in the world in 1901 called "Black Maria Production Company", six years before The Warner Brothers opened their Cascade Theater in New Castle, PA. In 1907. Thomas Alva Edison made short five to eight minute, one reel movies, for Vaudeville Theaters and peep shows. Not the type of peep shows that carry that label today; but, peep shows picturing The Statue of Liberty, The Grand Canyon or an Old Boxing Match. But, as luck would have it Edison's Production went out of business in 1903. Harris purchased the Nickelodeon Theater's projector from Thomas Edison which is now in the Senator John Heinz Museum in Pittsburgh. Harris needed a screen, which he made from muslin and chairs, 96 of them which he borrowed from high schools, funeral parlors, and St. Philips Catholic Church in

Crafton. He built the box office with the help of Big Ted West, the big Irish usher/bouncer, with a brogue so thick many Pittsburghers couldn't understand him.

The Nickelodeon was in a great location; but, Harris was a little concerned about the traffic on Smithfield Street. He thought the noise would bother the movie audience? The movies were silent of course; but, there was the organ and piano music. There still weren't many cars in Pittsburgh as a matter of fact they were forbidden on Smithfield Street. But, every once in a while one would come down the street. There were street cars pulled by horses, carriages pulled by horses and an occasional car that backfired and scared the hell out of the horses.

If the Pittsburgh police caught a car on Smithfield Street it would cost the driver not less than $25 or more than $100 and/or 60 days in the Allegheny County Workhouse (jail). The offense was called, "Operating a motor vehicle upon or over the streets of Pittsburgh". And we complain about the price of tickets today.

Well Harris had the theater almost ready to open. He had the projector, he got from Thomas Edison, and the 96 chairs he got from St. Phillips Catholic Church in Crafton, PA, the screen he made from muslin. However, nobody knows what the first features was. Even movie historians disagree. Some say it was a double feature, with the first movie made in England called, "The Baffled Burglar" and followed by the comedy "Poor But Honest" but, the production dates didn't jive. Others say it was "The Great Train Robbery" produced in 1903 and seen in peep shows on hand cranked view masters, produced two years before the Nickelodeon opened. However, my Mother always told us it was ,"The Great Train Robbery" that opened the Nickelodeon. But, she was only two years old when the Nickelodeon opened. So, I'm sure she heard it from her Father and I have to believe she was right.

There was still one important thing that had to decided upon before the theater opened and that was the name. The name of the theater, what was he going to call it? They had to know that, because they couldn't put a sign up until they had a name. Ted West had already started to build the marquee and left room for the name, whatever it was going to be called; but, they couldn't think of a name. Well in about a week of thinking and kicking it around with his friends, he decided upon a name, for the theater; He decided to call it the NICKELODEON, Nickel was the price of admission and Odeon was the old Greek word for theater, hence the Nickel Theater ....The Nickelodeon. Harris coined the name in June of 1905 and put it on the marque outside of the building and the rest is history.

The Nickelodeon became the most famous Theater in the world. Shortly after the Nickelodeon opened and because of its success, three thousand copy cat movie theaters appeared around the country. Including the Warner Brother's Cascade, in New Castle, PA, in 1907 and Louie B. Mayer's, The Gem formerly a Vaudeville theater. Mayer renamed it The Orpheum and it was located in Haverhill, Massachusetts. also in 1907.

The date was June 19, 1905 and the Nickelodeon opened showing, "The Great Train Robbery" or was it the double bill called "The Baffled Burglar" and "Poor But Honest" we'll probably never really know, I'll just say the first features was "The Great Train Robbery". However, we are sure the Edison Produced short movies such as: "The Ex-Convict" produced, in 1904; "The Kliptomaniac", produced, in 1905; and of course "The Great Train Robbery", produced in 1903; the 1897 Corbett-Fitzsimmons Championship fight and the 1899 Jeffries-Sharkey fight. These were the greatest fights of the time and all played at the Nickelodeon. However, on the Nickelodeon's opening day the crowd turn out was relatively small the first day June 19, 1905; but, Harris didn't loose hope. He knew as soon as the public knew about the Nickelodeon, business would boom and boom it did, on the second day. At 8 am on June 20th, 2,000, people stood in line to get into the Nickelodeon. I don't believe 2,000 people would stand in line to get into a theater today at 8am.

The Nickelodeon averaged between seven thousand and eight thousand people a day. It was opened from 8am to 12 midnight seven days a week and the shows would run about 15 to 20 minutes each, which ment a new house full every 20 minutes The Nickelodeon was so successful that in a short period of two years, there were 3,000 Nickelodeon copy-cat type theaters nation wide. All because of this one little theater on Smithfield Street, in Pittsburgh PA.

The Nickelodeon, June 19, 1905, Pittsburgh, PA

(There was never an actual photograph of the Nickelodeon or I haven't been able to find one. The theater opened in 1905 and was torn down in 1910. The picture on the cover of the book was touched up by El Paso Times illustrator and political cartoonist Nacho Garcia, no one seems to know where the original rendering came from.)

THE MOVIE POLICE

EVERYTHING IN THE MOVIE BUSINESS was new in 1905 because there was no movie business until then. The fear for women in dark rooms, mixing with strange men brought out the "movie police" organizations of local citizens trying to pass laws, because of men and women together in dark rooms. These organizations suggested the lights be turned on through out the whole movie, they also suggested that men sit on one side and women sit on the other side. There were concerns about emigrants who were attending the theater and in those days the emigrants were mostly Germans and Irish. There were concern about violence and sexual themes of the movies themselves……. So, what's new? Harris however, was way ahead of the "Movie Police". He had his 6'2" 220 pound Irish usher/bouncer on staff, who would watch for just such shenanigans, as he called them.

The projector used at the Nickelodeon had no take-up reel, so the film went through the film gate in front of the projector and into a bag at the bottom. This meant a lot of handling of the film itself, which was nitrate based and very flammable. A couple of the Nickelodeon copy-cat theaters, in Pittsburgh had film fires the projectionists were badly burned; but, fortunately there were no fatalities. The cause of many of the film fires was the lamp which illuminated the film. The heat from the lamp in many cases caused the highly flammable nitrate film to explode. Also, the person retrieving the film had to be very careful not to crease the film. It had to be rolled onto another reel, "heads out" and made ready for the next showing.

Business was so good and since there was no income tax, in those days Harris was making $300 to $400 a day, $2,800 a week equal to about $48,000.00 a week in todays money. The films were running about 15 or 20 minutes per showing. And there were anywhere from 6,500 to 7,500 people going through the Nickelodeon every day. That translates into a little more than $115,000.00 a year and that was in 1905 money with no taxes and from the one theater, about $2.4 million, in today's money. In time Harris had somewhere around 60 theaters. And in those days you could bring your own popcorn, candy or peanuts into the theater and get in to see the movie for a nickel.

GUESS WHO CAME TO THE NICKELODEON

RIGHT ACROSS FROM THE NICKELODEON, on Smithfield Street was Kaufman's Department Store (now Macy's Department Store) The 3rd floor window in the Men's Department was a good place to check out the action below, at the Nickelodeon and that's where Harry Warner worked selling men's suites. He was intrigued with the business at the theater every time he looked out of the window at the Nickelodeon. This is the business for me, he thought and he said it many times. Harry decided to go down and meet the owner of the Nickelodeon on his lunch break the next day.

The next day Harry skipped lunch and walked across the street and into the Nickelodeon and met Harris. He told Harris that he worked at Kaufman's and couldn't help but notice the great business the Nickelodeon was doing. He told Harris he thought this was the business for him and his brothers and asked Harris if he could bring his brothers down to meet him. Well, Harris liked nothing more than to talk about the Nickelodeon; so, he told Harry if you don't bring your brothers down, He'd never buy another suit at Kaufman's. Well Harry and Harris became friends and a few days later Harry showed up with two of his brothers, Sam and Abe. Harris gave them the De Lux tour and they all were duly impressed. In the next couple of weeks the brothers were there two or three times a week, asking more questions, because by their own admission they knew nothing about the movie business at that time. And as Harry told Harris earlier, "This is the business for me."

Finally one day after work Harry returned to the Nickelodeon and told Harris he found a location in New Castle, PA he thought would be great for their theater. He asked Harris if he would look at the location and help them put the Cascade together. That's the name the brothers decided on. Harris got Thomas Edison, to get the brothers an Edison Kinetoscope projector, that's where Harris got the ones for the Harris Family Vaudeville Theaters and the Nickelodeon years earlier. The screen was mainly made from muslin in those days and chairs were borrowed usually from the churches and funeral homes. Harris thought he knew how to build a box office; but, he was smart enough to have Ted West actually do it. He told Harry he would love to help them with the Cascade and for a couple of days a week for about a month Harris and Ted West made the trip to New Castle, PA and the Warner's Cascade Theater. Harris said he almost liked making the trip to New Castle because Ben Warner, Harry's Father always brought the best food. The Cascade opened in 1907 it was a tremendous success.

The Cascade is all but gone now, I went up to New Castle, PA to see it in 2006, when I was working in nearby Youngstown, OH for the ABC Television Affiliate. The Cascade is only a memory now, it's main wall is still up; but, the theater is history; however, if you look long and deep into the wall you can almost hear piano music coming from it. I stood there for a few minutes and I thought I could hear it....

The brothers built another theater in Youngstown, Ohio which was equally successful. Finally the brothers decided to get into the distribution business as well, so, they set up a motion picture distribution center in Pittsburgh, (The building is still there). That's why I always say, "If it wasn't for John P. Harris, Harry Warner would still be selling men's suits at Kaufman's in Pittsburgh and Sam and Abe would be making

Deli sandwiches at Ben Warner's in Youngstown and Jack would probably be in Jail." The truth is, unlike the Selznicks, the Warner's rarely mentioned Harris' help or contribution to their success, even though they were friends. However, one of Harris' sons John H. did become a Vice President of Warner Brothers in the 30's, for a few years. It about this time in 2006 I met Cass Warner, Harry Warner's Grand Daughter a Producer/Author and a lovely and knowledgeable lady whose book, "The Brothers Warner" I most certainly would recommend and I believe the book is soon to become a major Motion Picture. Cass is the President of "The Warner Sisters Motion Picture Co." in Hollywood.

It was about this time, the year was 1907 that Louis B. Mayer, in Havirhill, MA purchased "The Gem" a vaudeville theater remodeled it and called it "The Orpheum" and started showing full length motion pictures. It was the spark that ignited Metro-Goldwyn Mayer Studios, which ultimately became the most famous studio in Hollywood. Louis B. Mayer became the father -in-law of David O. Selznick, the Oscar winning Pittsburgh producer of "Gone with the Wind.". There were many stories about Mayer and his love of women some good and some bad. However. according to IMBd, actor/director Eric von Stroheim once told Mayer, "All women are whores" and Mayer replied, "Well, how about your Mother?" and punched von Stroheim right in the face. From that moment on Louie became my hero. Louis B. Mayer struck a deal with Producer/Director D.W. Griffith, for the exclusive rights to show "The Birth of a Nation" in New England for $25,000 and that netted him $100,000. That's what put him in the distribution business in New England, like the Warner Brothers got into in Pittsburgh.

There is also a story about Judy Garland's weight problem during the filming of, "The Wizzard of Oz", Louie put her on weight pills (Dexadrene) to keep her weight down and possibly starting her on a life long drug habit. Many people claim this is true including Mickey Rooney, her true friend.

I mentioned this in my book about Howard Hughes called "Howard Hughes-The Las Vegas Years: The Women, The Mormons, The Mafia" and it seems that drug abuse just followed her throughout her life. My brother and sister Denny and Eleanor, were skating in an ice show at the

Aladdin Hotel in Las Vegas in 1968 and one of the producers Phil Richards was also the make-up man, for Judy Garland who was performing at the Riviera Hotel. Phil asked me if I would like to go over to the Riviera and meet Judy and see her show. That was a no brainer; so, I went to the Riviera with Phil and when we entered Judy's dressing room, Judy was sitting at her make-up table eating mashed potatoes and drinking black coffee. She had two friends, who were force feeding her. She appeared so drunk I didn't see how she could do the show. I was introduced to her and she appeared so frail I thought she would break. She couldn't have weighed more than 90 pounds or stood more than 4'10". Later a stage hand took me up stairs to the light booth, where I was to watch the show. The overture started and I thought this is going to be a disaster, she could hardly talk or walk out of her dressing Room. As I was thinking about this the showroom announcer was heard, "Ladies and Gentlemen The Riviera Hotel proudly presents Miss Judy Garland" the applause was deafening and the orchestra broke through the acclamation with, "Somewhere over the Rainbow" Judy walked out on stage as coordinated as Olympic Champion and "Dancing with the Stars" winner Kristi Yamaguchi. She spoke and sung like she never had a drink. I couldn't believe it and to top it off, it was one best show I had ever seen. On the way back to the Aladdin I asked Phil if that was SOP for Judy and he said, "Yep, I don't know how she does it; but, she does it every night and she's been doing it every night for years." On the way home I couldn't help but wonder if Judy's behavior was the result of Louis B's weight solution...... drugs and alcohol!!! One thing I have to mention, I loved Judy's singing, acting and movies and still miss her today.

HARRY WARNER WAS RIGHT

Harry Warner said, "There were so many theaters In those days that someone has to be making product for them and someone would have to be distributing the films. So the the brothers moved back to Pittsburgh and opened the Duquesne Motion Picture Distributing Company, later called Warner Brothers Motion Picture Distributing Co. However, The Warner Bro's. weren't the first to get into the distribution business. In Pittsburgh's Hill District, not far from The Nickelodeon, was a distributing company called Metro Distributing Co. later called the Metro-Goldwyn-Meyer Motion Picture Company. The Warner Brothers, Harry, Sam and Abe as well as the Selznick's, Lewis, Myron, and David O. received their motion picture Baptism in Pittsburgh at the Nickelodeon Theater. However, the motion picture business moved east to New York and finally west to Hollywood and the city that gave birth to the motion picture theater industry, mostly was ignored. even by the city where it was born.

In July 2009 they were getting ready to tear down the Warner Brothers Distributing Company building, one of the very first film distributors in the country. It had been there for over a hundred years. And was actually a historical site in the Motion Picture Industry in the City of Pittsburgh. And through the efforts of a college student, named Dru Levinson, who produced a documentary, in 2009 it was declared a historical location and saved.

The brothers decided to get into the production business. So, they moved to New York. There were problems in New York, especially with Thomas Edison, who tried to trademark all motion pictures for himself. Well the brothers didn't want to deal with that. So, they moved to Los Angeles. They bought 40 acres on Sunset Blvd., in Hollywood the present home of Channel 5, KTLA-TV, Gene Autry's old television station. Gene bought KTLA-TV for approximately twelve million dollars and after a few weeks later he thought he got ripped off, So, he tried to get his money back but it was just impossible and for that I'm sure he's forever grateful because years later, he ended up selling the studio for a little more than half a Billion dollars. The 40 acres Harry Warner bought became too small. So, they moved again, this time to Barham Boulevard, in Burbank and that's where they are today. They called their new lot Warner Brothers Studios.

LEWIS, MYRON & DAVID O. SELZNICK

WELL, NOW WITH HARRY WARNER gone to New York, and Los Angeles it was getting a little lonely for Harris at the Nickelodeon, in Pittsburgh when all of a sudden a man appeared asking the same questions that Harry Warner used to ask. His name was Lewis Selznick and he owned a Jewelry store on Smithfield St., in Pittsburgh just a block up from the Nickelodeon. called 'Keystone Jewelers'.

Lewis Selznick also saw the opportunities and potential in the new theater and motion picture business. Lewis and his boys David and Myron were frequent visitors to the Nickelodeon. They were there practically every day. After about a year, Lewis decided to follow the lead of the Warner Brothers and head to Los Angeles. They wanted get into the business and did they ever get into it. Lewis became a major player in the studio marketing and production business, working for many of the major motion picture companies in California, as well as his own and the boys Myron and David became producers.

Myron became a producer and later a very successful agent. However, when Myron was still a young producer he had to get his Mother to sign contracts for him because of his age. He had not yet reached the age of majority and couldn't legally sign anyone to a contract... His brother David was winning one award after another including an Oscar for his production of the motion picture, "Gone With the Wind" You'll remember him as Producer David O. Selznick. A few of David's movies were "Little Women." "The Thin Man" "A Star is Born" among many others.

In his book "David O. Selznick's Hollywood" by Ronald Haver, Bonanza Books, New York copyright 1980. Selznick talks about John P. Harris and Harry Davis and the motion pictures he saw at the Nickelodeon. David O. Selznick said "Harris and Davis didn't know it; but, with the Nickelodeon they just made history". The Selznick's, were true friends of John P. Harris, particularly Lewis Selznick the father and his son David..

SAM WARNER MADE THE MOVIES TALK

In October of 1927 the Warner Brothers came out with the first motion picture with sound starring Al Jolson and called "The Jazz Singer". Mary Harris Sheridan, John P. Harris' daughter and my Mother told me a hundred times," When Grand Dad was helping the Warners in New Castle, Sam Warner told Grand Dad (John P. Harris) "Ya know one of these days these things are going to talk and were going to be in on it." Sam was right and because of him the movies did talk. It was his prime motivation, making the movies talk and Sam got little recognition for his work Finally after years of research he figured it out for the movie his brothers produced "The Jazz Singer" starring Al Jolson. But sadly the day before "The "The Jazz Singer" opened, the first movie with sound, the movie Sam had worked so hard on, synchronizing the audio to 24 frames a second. to match the lips of the actors. Sam Warner died, at 39 years of age. His brothers Harry and Abe said, "The Jazz Singer killed Sam".

This new sound thing caused quite a commotion in the movie production business. It changed everything. If anyone was the Father of talking pictures, it was SAM WARNER. Sam's wife an 18 year old Ziegfeld dancer turned actress at Paramount, named Lina Basquette. Lina tried her best to get Sam to sell his invention to Paramount for a lot of money, but Sam, unlike his brother Jack, was loyal to his brothers and kept the project, with the Warner Family. Author/Journalist Adela Rogers St. John who was a guest many times on, "Mid-Day L.A." seen on Channel 9 in Los Angeles, in the 1970's a show I often directed referred to Lina Basquette as "The Screen Tragedy Girl". Her life after Sam Warner, went straight down hill. One good thing she did was to give up their daughter to Harry Warner to raise as his own, for $300,000.

In the years that followed Lina Basquette went through many stormy affairs, two suicide attempts and eight marriages. Lina was also the half sister of Marge Champion of the dance team of Marge and Gower Champion. Two of the greatest dancer/choreographers in motion pictures and stage history. According to IMBd, Lina was Adolf Hitler's favorite actress. I guess she beat out Marlene Dietrich for the much sought after title of "The Favorite of the Furher"..........Oh Boy !!!

October 6, 1927, the motion picture "The Jazz Singer", was actually the first sound picture with synchronized voice sound. Although, "Don Juan" was actually first picture with sound , starring John Barrymore, also a Warner Bro's. film, it had the sounds of swords clicking and the "hummm" sounds of Barrymore's kissing scenes, 150 plus of them. But it had no narration or talk. "The Jazz Singer" had actual conversations in it, as well as singing. It was the first real "talkie." and the one that changed the motion picture business.

Irving Thalberg, Production Chief at Metro- Goldwyn Mayer Pictures, was leaving the premiere of "The Jazz Singer" was ask what he thought of the talking motion picture. He replied, "It's only a flash in the pan, a fad that will be gone tomorrow". But Irving really knew the truth and the truth was that if M.G.M. didn't get on the stick and produce movies with a sound track, it would be the end of M.G.M. Irving Thalberg was married to the famous actress Norma Shearer and as Production Chief of MGM, his opinion carried a lot of weight. He knew, when these "talkie things," as he called them caught on, all of the studios would be in BIG Trouble.

HOWARD HUGHES & "HELLS ANGELS"

So, Irving Thalberg and every other Studio head was hoping, beyond hope that the "talkies" were a failure. However, Billionaire Producer/ Director Howard Hughes saw the value in talkies almost immediately. This guy was unbelievable !!! At that time, Hughes was working on the final editing of the most expensive motion picture ever made, at that time called "Hell's Angels" starring Jean Harlow and Ben Lyons. Hughes had just completed shooting it. But after seeing the "Jazz Singer" Howard baffled the entire cast of, "Hell's Angels" as only Howard could, by calling the entire cast into studio 'A' and saying to them, "I'm going to have to do some re-shooting on "Hell's Angels" Ben Lyons one of the stars of "Hell's Angels" said, "How much are you going to re-shoot Mr. Hughes?" Howard was silent for a few seconds, he looked down at the floor, then up to Lyons and said, "Ben, I'll have to re-shoot the whole damn thing....only this time...... with sound !!!"

It was so quiet, in the studio, you could hear a mouse piss on cotton at 100 paces. Nobody ever spent so much money on a movie and then just tossed it. Noah Dietrich, Hughes' financial advisor and number two man at Hughes Tool Company, in Houston Texas, almost had apoplexy, figuratively speaking. He told Hughes that the Hughes Tool Company couldn't afford to finance the motion picture; but, Hughes told Detrich to mortgage what he had to, to get the money, and he would re-shoot "Hell's Angels" this time, with sound.

Everybody in the motion picture business was laughing at Hughes, especially Louis B. Mayer, who said to him, "Howard, you should take your oil money and go back home to Texas, while you still have some left." Well, They weren't laughing when the profits started coming in. "Hell's Angels" was the most successful multi-million dollar action packed motion picture in history, to that time and nominated for two Oscars. It made Jean Harlow a super star. And the gross receipts set a record for the next few years. Howard did better then double his investment. In those days half a million dollar investment in motion a picture was staggering and Hughes put $4,000,000.00 plus into "Hell's Angels." That's all he would admit to anyway. Some say it was more like Five Million.

RICK SEBAK, SANDRA SAGALA & MARY ROBINSON

My hunt for the movie "The Life of Buffalo Bill"

IN 2006 A MOVIE PLAYED on PBS in Pittsburgh WQED-TV and when Rick Sebak, a producer- director and host of many historical and local shows learned I was a relative and still alive, he sent me a copy of the 1908 movie and I'll always be grateful to Mr. Sebak. In 1910 , John P. Harris produced his second motion picture called, "The Life of Buffalo Bill" directed by John O'Brien and starring William F. Cody (The real Buffalo Bill). I've heard about the movie from my Mother; but, I just thought that after all of those years it went the way of the Titanic. I'm still looking for a copy of that movie …Now, listen to this it's almost eerie, as I said I was looking for a copy of my Grand Fathers movie called' "The Life of Buffalo Bill" and after six years, at the end of February 2013, with the help of Author Sandra K. Sagala of the Erie County Museum, in Erie, Pennsylvania and a true authority on Buffalo Bill. I have a copy of the movie, sent to me by Sandra Sagala's friend Mary Robinson of the Buffalo Bill Museum in

Cody, Wyoming, who found the movie. I am so grateful to both of these women.

Cody was a most unusual man, a pony express rider, an Indian scout, a Congressional Medal of Honor winner and an award winning rodeo producer, traveling the world over. He was an Army Colonel, a Showman, a real estate developer instrumental in the founding of Cody, Wyoming, an Actor and of all things,,,,,,,,,,,,, the NFL Buffalo Bills football team, was named after William Frederick "Buffalo Bill" Cody, in 1950.

HARRIS LOVED PITTSBURGH EVEN MORE THAN SHOW BIZ

JOHN P. HARRIS LOVED PITTSBURGH so much he built a home near his Father John A. Harris in Crafton, then his brothers Frank and Dennis and Sister Anna and her husband Chris all built in the same neighborhood as well. J.P. (The Nickelodeon Guy) stayed in Pittsburgh bringing the number of theaters he owned to about 60. They were located in Ohio, West Virginia, Detroit, New York and Pennsylvania. Harris was frequently asked why he didn't take off to Hollywood, like the Warner Brothers and the Selznicks and Harris would always say:

> "What does Hollywood have that Pittsburgh doesn't have except Palm Trees; We have three rivers, they have only one. We have four seasons and they have only one, We have real people and they have actors. I love Pittsburgh and that's why I live here.....".

Finally Harris ran for the Pennsylvania State Senate and won big. He couldn't run both the theaters and his job in the Senate. So, he turned the theaters over to his brother Frank Harris. He won a second term by a land slide and during his second term, Harris became ill during a joint House/Senate meeting. According to those that were there he appeared flush then very pale and collapsed to the floor. A doctor arrived in less than a minute; but, couldn't revive Senator Harris.

So, on January 26, 1926, at age 55, John P. Harris, a Pennsylvania State Senator, a lawyer and creator of the first all Motion Picture Theater in the world, The Nickelodeon, passed into the hands of his Heavenly Father, leaving his wife Eleanor Davis Harris, son John H. Harris, daughter Nell Harris (zur Horst); daughter Mary Harris (Sheridan); son Harry D. Harris and daughter Genevia Harris (Hahn); brothers: Frank and Dennis Harris and sisters Eleanor 'Ellie' Harris, Anne Harris Durham and Mary Harris Wurtz.

'Three Generations of the Harris Family' – circa early 1920s

Standing: (L to R) Ellie Harris (d/John A.) – Mary Harris Wurtz (d/John P.) – Alice and Dennis Harris (s/John A.) – Harry Harris (s/John P.) – Christopher Durham m Anna (seated) – Nell Harris)d/John P.) Johnny Harris (s/John P.) – Eleanor and John P. Harris (s/John A.) – Mary (Bun) Harris (d/John P.) Seated middle: (L to R) Cecilia (m Frank) holding baby Lucas May Harris – Bridget and John A. (senior) – Anna Harris Durham (d/John A.) m Christopher Durham – Frank Harris (s/John A.) holding Libby his oldest. Front: Frank's children – Genevieve and John P. (named after uncle) – Geneva Harris (d/John P.)

Pittsburgh showed how much they loved John P. Harris. His funeral was the largest that Pittsburgh had ever seen, at that time. His friend James J. "Jimmy" Walker, the Mayor of New York City, took a special train from New York to Pittsburgh. Jimmy Walker was so flamboyant, they made a Movie about him called, "Beau James" starring Bob Hope. There were 5000 mourners at St. Phillips Catholic Church, in Crafton, for the funeral Mass. However, the church couldn't accommodate more than a thousand people. So, extra police were called to help handle the crowds. All sixty of the Harris Theaters closed for three days to honor John P. Harris.

In the next couple of weeks John P. Harris' brother Frank Harris was elected to fill the unexpired term of John P. Harris, So John P's youngest brother Dennis Harris and John P.'s son John H. took over the reigns of the Harris Amusement Company. And great things were to happen.

CATHERINE VARIETY SHERIDAN FOUND AND THE VARIETY CLUB IS BORN

As Vice President and General Manager of the Harris Amusement Company, one of John H. Harris' jobs was to work in place of the theater managers on their days off. Harris was working for Manager John Hooley one November night in 1928, at the Sheridan Square Theater, on Liberty Avenue in Pittsburgh, when Gene, the head usher heard a baby cry. Both he and Harris looked around for the baby and found her under a seat. She was a one month old little girl, with a note pinned on her dress which read, exactly like this:

> "born november 29 carnegie, I cannot keep cost too much money got eight more my man got little job me wash clothes got big bills maybe someone take care God no want to kill big sin better someone take good home."

In 1928 when you found a baby, the baby was pretty much yours. There was no such thing as the Child Protective Services in those days. So, Harris took the baby home to his Mother, (It almost sounds phony; but, that's what it said on the copy I read)

In the next few days Harris rounded up ten men, many of whom worked for him. On October 10th 1928, John H. Harris became the first President of the Variety Club, it was the Variety Club that he started, no matter how much the new operators of the club try to involve themselves and other men saying they all founded it, THEY DIDN'T. Harris started it. It was an off shoot, of a club he already owned, called the 'Tea Bag Club'. Harris got ten men together, with the intent of raising money to support little Catherine Variety Sheridan. Catherine's mother gave her the name Catherine, that was the name that was on the note pinned on Catherine's clothes when Harris and Kelly found her, in the Sheridan Square Theater. Harris put nine men together to take care of little Catherine and to pay her expenses. Many of these men worked with Harris and for Harris, in the entertainment industry, all were or became members of the Variety Club, whose members informally adopted little Catherine. She was named Catherine by her Mother, Variety for the Variety Club and it's members who were supporting her and Sheridan because she was found in the Sheridan Square Theater, Hence: Catherine Variety Sheridan. John Harris' Mother couldn't stand to see Catherine go into an orphanage, even a nice place like Rosalia Foundling Home. But, she had five adult children of her own and thought she was too old to care for another young child Catherine's age. So, little Catherine was put with the nuns at Rosalia Foundling Home. Members of the 'Tea-Bag Club', now called the Variety Club, who informally adopted Catherine. These members spent week-ends with Catherine and Holidays as well.

This went on for almost five years. Catherine went from one house to another. Handed about like a prize trophy, never being able to have her own family, with a real Mom and Dad. John H. Harris' Mother, Eleanor Davis Harris had enough; so, she called her brother -in-law Dennis Harris, whose wife Alice called her brother Norman and his wife Gladys and they adopted Catherine. Her new parents changed Catherine's name to Joan and their last name was Riker; So, Catherine Variety Sheridan became Joan Riker and she grew up like a normal little girl, without the media and press attention, just like any other young girl. Joan "Catherine Variety Sheridan" Riker graduated from Cornell University with a BS and RN. She became a Lieutenant in the Navy Nurse Corps, serving in the Korean War. In Sigon, Vietnam, She met Lieutenant Commander Michael Mrlik and they were married in 1957 moving to Charleston, South Carolina and raised a family. Joan Riker Mrlik passed away in September of 1994, at the hospital in which she worked. The Medical University of South Carolina. Joan was recuperating from cancer; but, a blood clot in her leg, led to a massive hemorrhage in her brain. She was 65 years old. "Joan Mrlik was an inspiration to all who knew her and a wonderful wife and Mother". Monsignor John A. Simonin, the pastor of Saint Mary's Catholic Church, in Charlston, SC said, "Joan Riker Mrlik was cremated and her ashes were sent to Arlington National Cemetery".

The fact that John H. Harris and head usher Gene Kelly found the baby in the Sheridan Square Theater, the baby Catherine was turned over to Eleanor Harris originally and was finally adopted by Eleanor Harris' brother and sister-in-law is never mentioned by the Variety Club and I find that extremely strange. The fact that there has been no controversy for the first eighty years only leads me to believe that it's coming from Variety Club Members seeking their 15 minutes of fame and re-writing history.

A little more about the head usher at the Sheridan, the head usher at the Sheridan Square Theater, in East Liberty a section of Pittsburgh who was working with John Harris the night they both found Catherine Variety Sheridan decided to follow the Warner Brothers and the Selznicks to Los Angeles, to become a dancer. Well, he became a dancer all right and a choreographer, and a director, an actor and a producer. He was that, "Singing in the Rain" guy, a Pittsburgher named Gene Kelly

John Hooley was the manager of Sheridan Square Theater and not John Harris. This part is true, Harris never said he was the manager. He was the Vice President and General Manager, of the Harris Amusement Co. which owned the Sheridan Square Theater. And as Vice President and General Manager of all of the theaters one of his jobs was to relieve John

Hooley and other Harris theater managers on their days off. John Hooley had been the manager of the Sheridan Square, for some time, Catherine's mother could recognize John Hooley. She would call him every few weeks to check on Catherine; but, would never identify herself to Hooley, only to say she was Catherine's Mother. She never give him an address or phone number. She would always call from a pay phone that couldn't be traced by the police, because her calls were short enough to eliminate detection.

Others say Gene Kelly wasn't the head usher at the Sheridan Square, at that time. However, the Pittsburgh Post-Gazette Newspaper got it right in November of 1928 when it reported that John H. Harris and the head usher and Pitt (University of Pittsburgh) student Gene Kelly both found the baby, in the Sheridan Square Theater, in East Liberty. And that's the TRUTH.....Harris started the "Tea-Bag-Club" which morphed into the Variety Club and that's the TRUTH. Now, had Harris just given the baby Catherine to the City of Pittsburgh, to be put in an orphanage, like most suggested he do, instead of taking baby Catherine home to his Mother. THERE WOULD BE NO VARIETY CLUB today or whatever they call it now days. They changed the name of the Variety Club after 70 years. Can you imagine changing the name of the "OSCAR" to the to the "OSWALD" just the thought is ludicrous and foolish.. Now that Harris and Gene Kelly are both gone, It appears that someone is trying to re-write history; but, I'm not gone yet !!! And I'm not going to let it happen while I'm alive.

Dennis Harris, the uncle of John H. Harris, and Dennis' wife Alice Riker Harris (my great Aunt) were responsible for Alice's brother Norman and his wife Gladys Riker for adopting the baby Catherine and no one else.

The Variety Clubs of America still do a wonderful service for children and should be recognized and applauded, for their efforts. It's just that some of its members and employee and I know who they are, have tried to re-write history and include themselves, in the story in which they never belonged and never even knew.

HARRY HARRIS TAKES A WIFE

I**T WAS ABOUT THIS TIME** Harry Harris, John's younger brother met the daughter of magician Howard Thurston, from Columbus, Ohio. He eventually became the most famous magician of his time. Harry Houdini once said of Thurston, "Once he retires there will never be another like him." Harry Harris had the good looks of a movie star and many of Harry's friends in the business suggested that he follow that direction in life, especially since the family had all the connections. Harry had one problem though, he was afflicted, with the "Irish Curse" ALCOHOL. However, when he was sober he was the nicest guy you would want to meet. And Jane Thurston felt exactly that way. She never knew, Harry managed to hide the "Curse" from Jane and before you knew it they were married. Then it happened, Harry would get drunk, he would need money, for one of his binges. So, he would go to one of the Harris Theaters and threaten to fire the manager if he would not cash a check for him. He couldn't fire the manager anyway, but the manager didn't know that. He cashed thousands of dollars in checks, which John made good. Harry tried everything to stop drinking, religion, sobriety counselling centers and hospitals; but, nothing worked. Finely, Jane had enough and filed for divorce. Howard, Jane's father and Harry Harris got into a fight over Harry's relationship with his wife Jane and Howard pulled out a tear gas gun and shot Harris in the face, permanently blinding him in the left eye. The divorce became final; but, Harry could never stop drinking. John tried his best to help Harry, giving him jobs, giving him money but, again nothing worked. In 1956 John hired Harry as Promotion Director for Ice Capades International, later Ice Capades West Company The show was in Canada when Harry fell of the wagon again. He was walking back to the hotel from a local bar in the snow, when he suffered a heart attack and died at age 52. He was my uncle and when he was sober he was the greatest guy, full of fun, stories and full of life and that's the way I choose to remember him.

GENE KELLY & PAT O'BRIEN IN L.A.

IN THE MID AND LATE 70's I directed many of the national "Jack La Lanne Show" Shot at Channel 9, in Los Angeles I did news cut-ins and promotional spots as well as a show called "Mid-Day- L.A.", a two hour daily show, five days a week I often directed. The show had a lot of very famous guests, politicians, writers, actors and actresses, including Jane Fonda, Tom Hayden, Shirley MacLain, Jack Nickelson, Jacqueline Bisset, Jack Palance, George Peppard, Pat O'Brian, Gloria Swanson, Bill Conti, Silvester Stalone, Douglas Fairbanks, Jr., Tommy Lasorda, Roger Moore, Roman Gabriel and many more. Pronouncing a celebrities name wrong is really a no-no. So, we always did our best to get it right. One day Jack Palance was the guest on "Mid-Day- L.A." and the announcer Ted Meyers wasn't sure of the pronunciation of his names so he decided to go out into the Green Room and ask him. Ted was a religious man but not a hypocrite and even the stage hands tried not to swear around him. So, he walked out and said to Jack, " Jack I was wondering what the correct pronunciation of your name is?" Jack looked at Ted and said, "Who really gives a F--K" and Ted surprised everyone in the room by saying, "Well Jack, I really don't give a F--K how you pronounce your name, It's just that I'm the announcer here and I thought you would want me to say it properly but I'll just FU--ING guess." Jack actually apologized and said "It's like balance, that's how you remember it Jack Palance like balance." The same thing happened again only with me asking the pronunciation. The actress was one of the most beautiful women I've ever seen and that's why I probably did the questioning in the first place. Her name was Jacqueline Bisset. I always remembered her from the movie 'The Deep" Anyway, I asked her how to say her name and she gave me a real lesson, in genealogy telling me her family originally came from France and it was pronounced 'Bee-say' but after they got here, her family anglicized it to 'Biss-it' Then she looked directly into my eyes and said, "Here's how to remember it blue eye, Jacqueline Biss-it.....just like kiss it." Well, when she said that, I felt like somebody just kicked me in the chest, I told her I would make sure the announcer knew the correct pronunciation of her name. I turned around and staggered back into the control room. I didn't really care how to pronounce her name I just wanted to talk to her. Jack Nickelson was on the show one day and I noticed he had a little propeller pinned on his lapel; so, I said "Are you a pilot Jack?" and he said no and with that smile he made famous in "The Shining" he said, "It's just lapel art, isn't it great" I thought the old clock on the wall says that's all; so, I moved on.

One day we had Pat O'Brien as a guest on "Mid-Day L.A." I was sitting in the make-up room, with Danny Martinez one of the KHJ radio stars, from the station owned by R K O pictures and we were talking with make-up artist Bob Germaine and actor Pat O'Brien about the Ronald Reagan "Win One for the Gipper" speech.

Pat O'Brien played the coach, Knute Rockne in the 1940 movie: "Knute Rockne All American" with Ronald Reagan. O'Brien jumped out of the make-up chair and delivered his great movie speech as Knute Rockne. He had completed the Rockne speech, when who walks into the make-up room but Gene Kelly. " It's only me Irish chauffeur" said O'Brien. He and Pat were pals and Gene went to park the car. After everyone exchanged pleasantries I asked Gene if he remembered John Harris from Pittsburgh and he said, "Do you mean the theater guy that owned the Ice

Capades?"…… "That's the guy", I said, then Gene said," Believe it or not I used to work for him, in Pittsburgh, at The Sheridan Square when I was going to Pitt. He continued, Harris still lives in Pittsburgh and I've been to his house here in Beverly Hills, on Sunset Drive, I said "9940 Sunset" and Gene thought for a Second and said "that sounds right". Then Gene said," How did you know that, are you roping me into something?" Then I told him he was my uncle. I then reminded him about Catherine Variety Sheridan and he repeated the same story I've heard a thousand times; but, it was fun hearing it from him.

Gene became my new best friend, if only for a very short time. After the show at Channel 9 we had lunch at Nickodels, between Channel-9 and Paramount Studios. Gene died a few years later; but, I'll never forget him. And if I wasn't working for Channel 9 in Los Angeles, KCAL-TV. I would have never met him.

(Photo Credit: Compliments of skater Michael Garren of Ice Capades.)
Gene Kelly with cast members of Ice Capades

THE HARRIS AMUSEMENT CO. THE PITTSBURGH HORNETS AND THE DUQUESNE GARDENS

WITH THE EXCEPTION OF A few theaters, The Harris Theater Company was sold to the Warner Brothers on April 15th 1930 for $3,000,000. approximately $60 million in today's money. It was a little bit after "The Jazz Singer" and the Warner Brothers were trying to get as many theaters as possible, that could be wired for sound. Because that's where the movies were going after the "Jazz Singer". So, after a short stint with the Warner Brothers, as a Vice President, running their theaters in the east and midwest John H. Harris returned to Pittsburgh. He had a non compete clause in his (5) year contract so he had to stay out of the theater business for (3) more years. Harris was looking for something to do. He couldn't go back into the theater business for three more years, because of the non-compete clause, in his contract with the Warner Brothers.

One day John H. Harris drove out to the Oakland area to see the new Saint Paul's Cathedral, it had just recently been constructed and was a beautiful church. It still is today. You could say it was Pittsburgh's Saint

Patrick's Cathedral. And just across the street from the church, standing in stark contrast, to the beauty of the Cathedral was an old dilapidated trolly barn, where they stored many of Pittsburgh's street cars. It was a very large building built in 1890 as a street car barn and now, it was for sale or rent. Harris knew he could do something with it. He walked into the barn, it was very dark and eerie but, he knew he could do something with it; but, he didn't know what:

In 1895 it became an ice rink home of the NHL Pirates from 1925-1929; The Western Pennsylvania Hockey League's 'Yellow Jackets' ; followed (1915-1925/1930-1932); then The Shamrocks (1935-1936) then not much happened.

Then one day it came to Harris, Pittsburgh didn't have a sports arena; so, this could be it. There were no pillars, blocking the audiences view and this was important for a sports arena. Can you imagine having pillers in the middle of a basketball court or a hockey arena. So, Harris decided to take over the trolly barn. It was the largest one story building in Pittsburgh, that was capable of housing; rodeos basketball, hockey and ice skating. He called it The Duquesne Gardens.

Harris built a large marquee out in front of the building, beautiful concession stands and seats and boxes for the spectators. He built one of the largest ice surfaces, in the country for hockey and public skating. He knew the ice skating crowd wasn't enough to support the investment. So, he started to look for additional business opportunities, shows and events he could book into Duquesne Gardens. In Detroit he became aware of the Detroit Olympics of the International American Hockey League, and he learned they were for sale. He was intrigued with their speed and their ability to hit hard. John was a sports guy and loved hockey, he couldn't get the Detroit Olympics out of his mind; but, a hockey team, It was a full time job, to run one of those teams. So, he thought and thought about it and finally he bought the team. He relocated it to Pittsburgh and changed its name to the Pittsburgh Hornets and the league changed its name to the American Hockey League. Most teams were using wire mesh screens to protect the fans from a wild puck; so, The Pittsburgh Plate Glass Company was the first to develop a shatterproof glass called Herculite and nobody could watch a game better than a Pittsburgher. It was known in the hockey world at that time that Pittsburgh had the biggest ice surface and best ice.

The Hornets thrilled their new home town Pittsburgh fans by winning their very first game against the tough Cleveland Barons by a score of 5 to 2. on November 8, 1936. Remember these were depression times and money was very scares, the price for a single admission ticket was 35 cents and the box seats went for 75 cents. Nothing like the $65. to $300. tickets price today. However, the players were only getting between $25,000 to $50,00 not the $700,000 to $4,500,000 or more a year the players get today. The Hornets turned out to be one of the great teams in the American Hockey League winning three Calder Cups, the American Hockey League equivalent to the Stanley Cup in the National Hockey League.

The Hornets beat the Cleveland Barons in 1936; the Providence Reds in 1952 and the Buffalo Bisons in 1955, to win their three Caulder Cups. John H. Harris owned the Pittsburgh Hornets from 1933 to 1956, That's when they tore down the Duquesne Gardens. A few years, later the Hornets carried on under new ownership; but, they were never the same old team. And when the Penguins came to Pittsburgh, it was over for the Hornets. My brother Thomas Sheridan worked for the Pittsburgh Hornets for a few years after they moved to the Civic Arena, as the Promotion and Marketing man. But he said there were new players, a new arena and he felt that the excitement, that was always with the Hornets, at the old Duquesne Gardens was no longer there. Even after winning the Calder Cup in 1967 the team just vanished. Tom was right. The Old Hornets were gone and the New Hornets were never the same.

The Duquesne Gardens, Pittsburgh, PA

The Pittsburgh Hornets, with Owner John H. Harris in the suit next to number 3.

PITTSBURGH'S FIRST AND ONLY NBA TEAM

I'LL BET YOU NEVER KNEW John H. Harris brought an NBA Basketball team to Pittsburgh. Well he did and they were called The Pittsburgh Ironmen. The Ironmen were members of the BAA, Basketball Association of America which merged into the NBA, The National Basketball Association in 1949. It's been said that the team's defense was on THE WRONG SIDE OF MEDIOCRE. The team had piled up a terrible 15 and 45 record and finished dead last in the standings. However, Pittsburgh has the distinction of making the worst pick in the leagues very first draft. They choose Clifton Mc Neely a 28 year old Army Veteran from Texas. Unfortunately, nobody bothered to ask him the question, "Do you want to play professional basketball?" Well, he didn't and McNeely turned down the Ironmen in favor of staying at home and getting a job coaching high school basketball. It appears the draft interview process was not very rigid in those days. As it turned out the draft wasn't so great for the Ironmen period. As history will note, the best evidence the Ironmen ever existed comes from their embarrassing showing in the team's one and only draft.

In spite of everything, the Ironmen had some very distinguished alumni in John Abramovic, Stan Noszka, Colby Gunther (leading scorer), Press Maravich: later a college coach and father of the great Pete (Pistol Pete) Maravich and finally Red Mihalik, he played in only seven games, but was more famous as a Hall of Fame Referee.

Team owner John H. Harris finally pulled the plug and it was lights out for the Ironmen, before the start of the 1947-48 season. Their .367 winning percentage remains the second worst in NBA history.

JOHN H. HARRIS TAKES A BRIDE

IN THE EARLY 1930's HARRIS was spending much of his time on the West Coast with his pal actor George O'Brien, who was a favorite of Director John Ford. They were all Irish, including Harris and they used to tell old Irish stories and just reminisce. about the old country. John Ford's real name was Sean O' Feeney. As a matter of fact George O'Brien's last movie was for John Ford in 1964, in the movie "Cheyenne Autum". Harris' Grand Father, John A. came from County Cork, Ireland and his Grand mother Bridget Gaughan was from Limerick, Ireland. Harris knew he was related to actor Richard Harris and to the day he died couldn't figure out how.

George O'Brien was a Navy boxing Champ and was decorated for bravery a number of times during in World War l. He was a graduate of University of California at Santa Clara. George O'Brien became so close to the Harris family he was like an honorary brother.

*John H. Harris (White Hat), unknown,
Actor George O'Brien (Black Hat), unknown
Circa 1932 Warner Brother's Studios Hollywood*

As I said Harris and O'Brien were really pals; but, there were other reasons for Harris' repeated trips to the West Coast. The other reason was to see O'Brien's girl friend's, girl friend Lucille Williams. After his frequent visits to Malibu and her frequent visits to Pittsburgh, She accompanied the Harris Family to France, before Hitler came marching down the Champs Elysees into Paris. They went to Greece to visit Producer Spyros Skouras a major stock holder and owner of 20th Century Fox, then Skouras took them to Egypt to see the Pyramids, before German Field Marshall Ervin Romel got there, with his tanks. In Honolulu, they met with John's old pal Gold Metal Olympic Champ, swimmer Duke Kawanamoko, before the Japanese dropped their calling cards on Pearl Harbor. It seems they were one step ahead of the wolves all the way; but they had a great time.....

John H. Harris and Lucille Williams married January 22, 1932. In the summer of 1933. John and Lucille visited Nice, France because she loved France so much. They returned to Pittsburgh, three months later and just about a year later, they adopted a baby boy from the Roselia Founding

Home, the same home where Catherine Variety Sheridan lived earlier, they named the baby John H. Harris ll. There were problems from day one. He was a hard child to manage Johnny didn't like rules. And he felt he could do anything he wanted to do. In spite of everything. He was sent to the best schools, had plenty of money and a car in high school. He had permission to use his father's membership in the best clubs. But, he never had a close relationship with his father. I don't know where the blame lies. I just know his Father was a hard man to have any kind of relationship with. He was a type 'A' personality, always too busy with paper work or in meetings or dealing with people; but, he was never the type of person to sit down with or just have a real one on one conversation. It was usually his way or the highway. On the other hand, Johnny was a hard guy to handle. Johnny was sent to a military schools when his parents divorced, in 1943. He attended St. Johns Military Academy in Santa Monica. Then he went away to high school, ending up in his senior year, living with his Aunt (Bun) Mary and Uncle Andy, The Sheridans, in Pittsburgh,

John Jr. had trouble getting along with people everywhere he went and I'm not sure if it was all his fault. However, he felt he was entitled to an executive position with the Hornets, Ice Capades or in the Harris Amusement Co., Not because of ability; but, because, of who his adopted-father was. He was always telling people, "Do you know who I am. I'm John H. Harris ll". More about John H. Harris ll later.

THE DUQUESNE GARDENS AND SPORTS

JOHN H. HARRIS HAD THE Duquesne Gardens in the black in no time. The Hockey team brought more skaters into the building. The walls of the Gardens lobby, were filled with pictures of hockey player, and figure skaters and those who have appeared at the Gardens, like wrestlers The Great Don Eagle, Farmer Don Marlon and Gorgeous George, as well as Ice Capades and Ice Follies skaters.

Harris brought boxing to the Gardens with Billy Conn and Fritzie Zivic both Pittsburghers and both world champions. He brought bicycle races and rodeos with The singing Cowboys Gene Autry and Roy Rogers and Jock Mahoney (The Range Rider) actress Sally Field's Step Dad to the Gardens. Buster Crabb and the Aqua-Parade (Buster was Tarzan, in the movies right after Johnny Weismuller). But Pittsburghers loved the Hornets like they love the Penguins and Steelers today. I think they even love the Pittsburgh Pirates, It's just that they just don't talk about them too much right now; but, they are beginning to do better. Only remembering they were the first team in the World Series and the only MLB team still playing. And what Pittsburgher could forget the great Ralph

Kiner who almost broke Babe Ruth's home run record with 59 home runs in the days before steroids and other performance drugs. And who could ever forget , Bill Mazeroski's World Series winning home run against the Yankees, in 1960, to win the World Series. Coming from Pittsburgh, I'll never forget that run. I was sitting in the cafeteria at Phoenix College, in Phoenix, Arizona watching the World Series, in stead of going to class and saw Bill Mazeroski hit that home run. I even have an autographed picture of Mazeroski rounding third and heading home.

Believe it or not, the biggest sports guy I ever knew, I mean this guy really loved sports. He was an L.A. Dodger named Lasorda, a Pennsylvanian at that, figure that out and there will never be another one like Lasorda...... NEVER!!! There was a time when Lasorda was the manager of the Albuquerque Dukes, the Dodger farm team, in New Mexico, Before he became manager of the Los Angeles Dodgers. Steve Yeager, one of the great Dodgers, was in the outfield. After practice Lasorda called Yeager over and said to him ,"Steve, tomorrow I want you to dress for catcher." Steve said , "I'm an outfielder Skipper, I'm not a catcher." Lasorda said, "Steve all of the really great catchers started as outfielders like Johnny Roseborough, Roy Campenella, Mel Ott and you're in their class, So, tomorrow dress for catcher." Steve said, "O.K. Skipper" and walked off the field. Rick Monday heard the whole conversation and said to Lasorda, "Hey, Skipper those guys you named to Yeager were never outfielders, they were always catchers." Lasorda looked at Monday and said, "I know that, you know that BUT YEAGER DON'T KNOW THAT." As it turned out Lasorda was right Yeager didn't know that ; but, he became one of the greatest catchers in baseball, when moved up to the Los Angeles Dodgers.

Steve and I became friends during that time. We worked on a few television pilots, with Tommy Lasorda and Roman Gabriel, the great L.A. Rams quarterback. Then one night at dinner at Steve's house he mentioned that he had a reading at Universal Pictures the next day. He was getting quite a few acting jobs then and I think that's what he wanted to do when he left baseball. Anyway, I ran into Steve a few days later and asked him how the Universal thing went. He looked at me and said, "You're not going to believe this Pal; I turned the job down" I said "What happened? They wanted you to do a nude scene" Steve said, "Worse than that. They wanted me to be a tough bouncer in a gay bar and at the end of the movie, you find out that I'm gay and the boyfriend of the owner of the bar. Well Jesus Christ, I couldn't let my Little Leaguers see me acting gay; so, I turned the damn thing down!" That's the way it is with Steve. Don't ask him a question if you don't want to know exactly how he feels about a subject and that's what I liked about him, what you saw is exactly what you got..

PITTSBURGH'S MOST BELOVED HOCKEY TEAM

THE PITTSBURGH HORNETS HOCKEY PLAYERS were always available to talk with and even play a little hockey with the kids, not like today. There were players like Tim Horton, Pete Backer, Leo Boivin, Gordie Hannigan and Ray Hannigan, Tim Costello, Sid Smith, Bill Ezinike, Sid Able, George "The Chief" Armstrong, John Ashley, Baz Bastien, who later became the Pittsburgh Hornet's coach, Gil Mayer Bob Solinger, Earl Balfor and Frank Mathers. These are just some of the guys I remember. I can't name them all; but, they were the greatest guys to ever lace up skates. The team was so tough they got two priests to pray for them. Ray Hannigan and Tim Costello both became Roman Catholic priests when they retired from hockey. After he was ordained, Tim, now Father Costello played for the 'Skating Fathers' in Canada and Ray, Father Hannigan prayed for them all. Most of those guys went to the NHL and six of them are now, in the Hall of Fame.

I have to take a few seconds to tell you about Tim Horton, my hockey hero. To this day, every morning I drink coffee out of my Tim Horton coffee cup. And whenever I get a chance, I drive up to Tim Hortons Coffee

Shop in Trail, British Columbia, Canada about 20 minutes from my son John's little ranch in Kettle Falls, WA. and talk about Tim, with Manager Devon Sims and at the Arena with Big Al Gywrache, Bruce Taylor and John Hudak, all old hockey players and former RCMP members, as well as Devon Sims father Gord Sims, still in the RCMP.

    I met Tim Horton when I was 12. He was playing for the Pittsburgh Hornets, in the American Hockey League. He was the toughest and best defense man, on the team. When I was 15, I would go to my Ice Capades Class practice just as the Hornets were finishing up their practice and Tim would always play a little hockey with me, passing me the puck; but, never checking me or I would probably be dead by now. I would chase him up the ice and he would pass me the puck, to shoot into the net and if I made it, he was happier than I was. We didn't do this very often maybe a couple times a month; but, I'll never forget it. It was almost like Sandy Kofax throwing the ball to a kid who wanted to be a catcher. I'll never forget Tim Horton, he was my Sandy Kofax. Later on, I went into Ice Capades and Tim moved up to the Toronto Maple Leafs of the NHL a power house in those days, winning (4) Stanley Cups and was a member of (6) All Star Teams, finally ending up with the Buffalo Sabers. Tim was killed at age 44 in 1974 in a car wreck in St. Catherines, Onterio Canada. But not before starting the largest and best, fast food restaurant chain in Canada, with (2,700) restaurants and with (80) stores in the United States as well, all called "Tim Hortons". Tim and his wife Lori, a former Pittsburgher, had four daughters. Lori joined Tim in Heaven in 2000. I almost forgot: The Canadian Broadcasting Corporation, lists Tim Horton, Number 59 on the list of the "Greatest Canadians". I would have moved him up about 58 spots. Tim Horton was a big tough guy; but, never too big and never too tough to help someone small. As long as I live, I'll never forget Tim Horton

Tim Hortons coffee cup

Most Arenas have rats in them but, the Duquesne Gardens had a little more than its share of rats, I'm talking about the four legged kind. There were plenty of the others. The hockey players used to try and shoot them with a puck. One point if the rat was stationary and two points if the rat was moving. One of the hockey players, who was afraid of rats, I won't mention Bill's name. But Bill brought his wife's mean tom-cat down to the dressing room. He thought that he would leave the cat there all night, and as big as it was it would serve as an eviction notice to the rats. The next morning not a trace of the cat remained. His milk dish was still there untouched. Most of the players felt that the cat met with a tragic fate. Rats made Bill so nervous he wore rubber shoes in the dressing room at all times, even into the shower. The guys that worked at the Garden's Mike and Joe Cancel, George and Clair and the skate shop Manager Reg Davies believe it or not, actually knew the rats by name. One day a group of us was standing by the Nevel Street goal net, just after hockey practice. The Nevel Street goal was the farthest one from the Gardens entrance. Reg Davies spotted a rat called Leonard. Reg had an ice pick in his hand because he had just installed one of the goals, he said, "Watch this I'm going to scare Leonard" and with that he throws the ice pick at Leonard which went right through Leonards mid-section, killing him immediately. Gordie Hannigan, one of the hockey players yells out, "Davies just got three points for icing Leonard."....... Icing a hockey term, that requires the game to be stopped and a face off the occur.

My brothers Tom and Harry and I, were away at boarding school at Mt. Gallitzin Academy, in Baden, PA bedtime was at 8:30pm; but, during hockey season the nuns would let us stay up on hockey nights and listen to Joe Tucker and the Pittsburgh Hornets games. Joe Tucker was the greatest, he could bring the game to life and next to being at the Duquesne Gardens and watching the action in person, listening to Joe Tucker was the next best thing. Joe's assistant for a couple of years became famous as the voice of the Pittsburgh Pirates. His name was Bob Prince and he replaced, "Aunt Minnie open the Window" Rosey Rosewell, who for years called the Pirates games. Whenever I think of The Pittsburgh Hornets, I can't help but think of the greatest hockey play-by-play announcer ever..... Joe Tucker and after all these years I still miss hearing him.

THE START OF ICE CAPADES

IN THE EARLY DAYS HOCKEY attendance was starting to fall off a little, not much but John Harris was thinking of ways to improve the crowd. Bingo !!! He got an Idea. He would bring a girl skater over to see if it helped with the crowd. So, in 1939 he hired a girl to skate between the periods, for one night. She skated alright right into the hearts of the audience. The girl was the three time Olympic Champion Sonja Henie. Sonja was just starting to become popular and Darryl F. Zanick of 20th Century Fox signed her to do some ice skating movies. She was the youngest girl ever to win Olympic gold, three of them. That is until 1998 when15 year old Tara Lapinski came along from Sugarland, Texas and beat Sonja's record by two months. Signing Sonja Henie turned out to be an expensive and costly evening for Harris. The audience loved her so much that they didn't go out to buy peanuts. popcorn, hot dogs and cokes. They just sat there and watched Sonja skate. In later years, Sonja became a major motion picture star and millionaire businesswoman.

'Olympic Gold Medalist Tara Lapinski and 8 year old Brendan Sheridan. Believe it or not that little guy, as of May 2013, became a police officer in Ohio.'

Sonja Henie and Michael Kirby

One night John H. Harris was talking to Jim Balmer a Harris Amusement Co. Executive. He told Balmer he hired Sonja Henie for one night at the Gardens. Harris asked Balmer what he thought he should pay her, Balmer said $150. maybe $100. More than $150 and you would be crazy.""You're looking at an insane man." said Harris" I just signed her for $2,500.00 and 50% of the gross. They didn't realize it then; but, they got a deal.

Signing Sonja to skate that night gave Harris a few ideas. He noticed how the audience loved to watch Sonja skate, even the hockey players came out early to watch her skate. Now whether these mean ole hockey players came out early, to watch Sonja's beautiful axel or just admire her lovlieness, I'll leave to you This made John H. Harris think about creating an ice show. An ice show with single skaters, pair skaters, comedy teams with a great chorus line, patterned after the New York City Rockettes or the Ziegfeld girls. On top of that he wanted each show to tell a story. He wanted a precision chorus line to be made up of boys and girls, 24 each who he later called Ice Capets and Ice Cadets and he wanted it to be the most spectacular chorus line in the business AND IT WAS..........

In the late 40's or early 50's, Ice Capades salutes the Royal Canadian Mounted Police

It Started With the Nickelodeon

Audiences loved the precision of a chorus line. Harris thought an ice show should tell a story like, "Cinderella", "Snow White" "Walt Disney's Toy Shop,""The Student Prince," "Brigadoon" even "Peter Pan" and the more he thought about it the more excited he became. An ice show that tells a story, much like a Broadway Show with a live orchestra, that was an important part of it. To tell a story, with great entertainment, with figure skaters and speed skaters and comedians; but, it was just a dream. So, he put it out of his mind for a while. But, every time he went down to the Duquesne Gardens and watched the ice skaters or saw a hockey game the thought came back to haunt him.

Then one day he booked an ice show at the Duquesne Gardens, produced by his friends Roy and Eddie Shipstead and Oscar Johnson it was called Ice Follies and was a spectacular show. Harris loved it; but, he felt with a story line like "Snow White," "Cinderella" etc. It would improve the entertainment value and appeal more to the families. And in 1948 Harris signed an agreement with Walt Disney and Cinderella became an ice skater.

'Donna Atwood and Bobby Specht In Ice Capades Cinderella'

So, Harris finally made up his mind. He was going into the ice show business and as soon as possible. He hired Rosemary Steward and Bob Dench, English Olympic Champions and a husband and wife team. There job was to teach the chorus kids (line kids) routines, as well as to help coach the principles and skate in the show as well. Harris hired Belita, Vera Hruba (Ralston) and Lois Dworshak as the stars. Trixie, was a star as well, with an unusual act. She skated and did acrobatics as well as juggling. Her husband was also included in the act . He was Esco LaRue. Esco was a plant who was seated in the audience and during her number he appeared drunk and would yell out, "That's not so great, I could do that" Then he would walk out onto the ice slipping and falling everyone thought he was drunk, he would try to dance with Trixie, he would grab her hand and ankle and swing her around, like skaters do. Well, you know the old saying, "You had to be there!!!" Believe me it was funny. Harris also hired a very smooth stilt skater, who was superb, his name was Phil Taylor he was the Father of World Champion Megan Taylor, who skated for a short time with Ice Capades. Phil later went into management with the show.

Phil Taylor, father of World Champion Megan Taylor

It Started With the Nickelodeon

Harris also hired two of the best all around management people in the business. They were skaters, refrigeration engineers, Zamboni mechanics, skate sharpeners and more. If anything needed to be taken care of, in the show these guys could do it. And they could skate in the show as well. They were two Pittsburghers; Joe Setta (Ursetta) and Bob Skrak. Joe was a principle and line skater and Bob was a line skater. I don't think you could produce a show today without guys like Joe (Setta) Ursetta and Bob Skrak. Joe Setta's wife Pat Huber Yeates Setta also skated in the show; but, left to be in the movie "Snow White and the Three Stooges" with Carole Heiss, Edson Stroll and The Three Stooges. Pat Huber was a beautiful girl and a graduate of the Ice Capades Training Class in Pittsburgh. Her husband Joe Setta (Ursetta) went on to own an arena in West Covina and later managed the rink in Culver City and Skrak owns a few arenas in Northern California.

'Donna Atwood taking a ride on the Zamboni and Bob Skrak at the controls'

*Jerry Mayhall, Ice Capades Music Conductor and
John H. Harris, President & Producer*

Stein and Castle, were two guys that always brought down the house Chuckie Stein was with Ice Capades Inc. and Paul Castle was with Ice Cycles later Ice Capades International and finally Ice Capades, West Company. Both were little people, sometimes called midgets. Each was a great skater as well as a marvelous entertainer. And believe it or not, everybody in the show looked UP to them, and in more ways than one...... Paul Castle left the show in 1955 to become the first Mickey Mouse in Disneyland and a life long friend of Walt Disney.

Comedian Jack Benny and Ice Capades President and Founder John H. Harris.

Rosemary Henderson: Ice Capades star and Wendy in 'Peter Pan' 1956

This Ice Show was a very expensive proposition, more than Harris had thought. The sets, the chorus line, the stars, the orchestra, the stage hands, the arena rental, the transportation all cost big money and Harris needed some help, to start his show; so, he decided to call on the his pal Walter Brown of the Arena Managers Association of which, Harris was a member, because of owning the Duquesne Gardens, in Pittsburgh. Harris struck a financial deal with the Arena Managers Association: Walter Brown, Owner of the Boston Gardens, the NHL Boston Bruins and the NBA Boston Celtics became Vice President; Lou Pieri, from Providence became secretary; Eddie Shore the great NHL Hall of Fame player from Springfield, MA became a Director; The others were John Sollenberger, from Hershey; Nathen Podoloff, from New Heven; Al Sutphin, from Cleveland, Lou Jacobs of Buffalo and Peter Tyrell from Philadelphia.

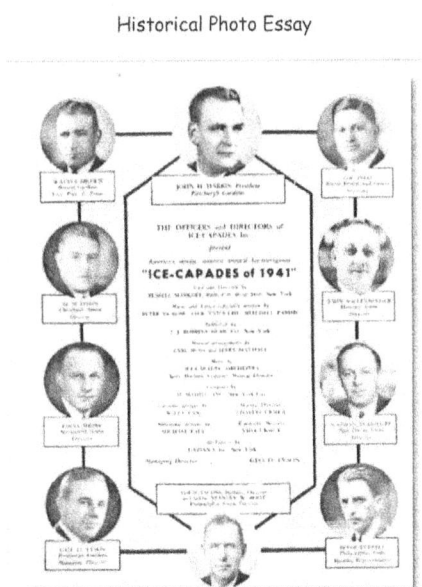

Members of the Arena Managers Assn.

It Started With the Nickelodeon

There were many good things about selling stock to the Arena Managers Assn. The men who made up the association many of whom knew skating, they also controlled the dates available, the play dates for the show. If you were in Cleveland you wouldn't want your next date to be in California (3000 miles away). You would be looking at Columbus or Hershey or even Cincinnati. The Arena Managers Assn. eliminated this problem.

They actually did a movie in 1941 called, believe it or not, "Ice Capades" starring Belita, Phil Silvers and Vera Hruba Ralston and Jerry Colona. It was even nominated for an Academy Award. They did a remake a year later, which also met with success. Now, Vera Hruba Ralston was a great skater; but, a so-so actress. She married Colonel Herbert Yeates, the owner of Republic Studios. The Colonel put her in one movie after another, trying to make another Sonja Henie out of her. She just couldn't act that well. After doing a couple of movies with Vera even John Wayne threw up his hands. "She was a wonderful person and a beautiful girl; but, the poor thing just can't act". There is a funny story relating to her name. There was another actress named Vera Ralston who Howard Hughes was insane about. Hughes assigned a car and driver to her and was trying to get her under personal contract. Well you'll never guess what happened. Vera and the driver fell in love and ran off and got married. Hughes was so mad he told Bill Gay in his L.A. office, the man who did all the hiring, that from then on he was to hire only homosexual drivers; but, this never happened, as far as we know. When Vera married the driver she changed her name to her husband's name, Miles. She became known as Vera Miles and was a major star. Vera Miles, Tippi Hedren and Grace Kelly were director Alferd Hitchcock favorite actresses. They all became major 'A' list stars and Hitchcock never let them alone.

Harris hired Red McCarthy one of the most exciting skaters in the show. He wore racing skates and jumped through rotating hoops of fire, over barrels and jeeps. He was the most spectacular act I've ever seen. I still remember him and I was only 4 years old. One of the most entertaining acts of all was Hugh Forgie and Stig Larson. They were badminton champions, in real life. Hugh was a World Champion many times over and Stig was a U.S. Champion. It was badminton like I've never seen before or since. It was funny, entertaining and it kept you in awe. Wondering how they could ever do that on ice. And they did it for close to 20 years. John hired Aja Zanova, two time World Champion and a delight to watch. There was the great team of Jackson and Lynam, Larry Jackson and Bernie Lynam two funnier guys never put on skates. Bernie was the quiet guy; but, he was my favorite, because he was just the opposite on the ice. There was Helen Davidson she was the real definition of the word elegance and always did the opening act, closing her number with a death spiral. There was the exciting and beautiful Jenny Baxter; Two time World Champion and U.S. Olympic Gold Medalist Dick Buttton, Patti Phillippi, French and World Champion Jacqueline du Bief, Jacqueline had one of the most exciting exits in Ice Capades history. As her number was ending, she would skate down ice toward the set at a tremendous speed and do a flying split jump through the curtains. The stagehands had to be on alert because as she came down the ice they had to open the curtains, about three feet, for Jacqueline's exit, through those curtains. God help the local stagehand that just happened to be walking past the open curtains at that time. Don't wory, It never happened.

Hugh Forgie, World Badminton Champion and Stig Larson, USA Badminton Champion, meet with celebrities opening night in L.A. You might not believe it; but, they were one of the best acts on ice.

Comedian Willie Kall and actress Joan Crawford at opening night in L.A..

*If it wasn't for Donna Atwood & Bobby Specht Actor
Joe E. Brown would have fallen on his ice.*

Rosemary Henderson showing Henry Seguin her engagement ring.

Bobby Specht, Ronnie Robertson, Cathy Machado, Henry Seguin and Richie Egan getting ready to go into the finale.

Bobby and Ruby Maxson were the brother and sister team who the audience just loved. They even got standing ovations in a place like Madison Square Gardens every night. When Ruby retired to get married and raise a family in the mid-fifties. Canadian champion the beautiful Rosemary Henderson took Ruby's place. She was as cute as can be and they called the act Rosemary and Bobby Maxson. I think a little poetic license was taken here, because Rosemary and Bobby weren't related. Bobby later married Helen Davidson, one of the principal skaters and they stayed with the show for 20 years plus. And how could I ever forget Eric Waite, 'The Clown Prince of Ice' Eric was just plain funny in skates or in shoes…..he just made you laugh. Rosemary Henderson also did a solo as a Canadian Champion, she was Wendy in "Peter Pan" as well and could act as well as any award winning actress.

Barbara Ann Scott also became a member of the Ice Capades Family when she replaced John H. Harris' wife Donna Atwood, who went on maternity leave, to have her twin boys. Barbara Ann Scott was a one of a kind Champion, talented, beautiful and the only Canadian woman ever to win Gold in the Olympics.

'Jenny Baxter, Jacqueline du Bief and Sonya Klopfer. Three of our best beach Capets….'

Jenny Baxter at work.

And how could any skater or audience member forget the greatest of them all, Comedian Freddie Trenkler. Not only was he hilarious on skates; but, probably one of the nicest men to ever put them on. Freddie married Gigi Naboudet a French Champion and Ice Capades skater and after years of a happy marriage God called Freddie home to entertain the Angels. Their daughter Margaret Trenkler Ramponi also skated in Ice Capades.

"Freddie Trenkler" The Greatest comedian of them all.

GiGi Naboudet Trenkler, French Champion

We also had two company cars an Isetta and a Messerschmitt. I wonder how many cast members remember them, maybe my long time friend Claudia Lattin a former Ice Capet would remember, she remembers everything. These were the most unusual cars I've ever seen. The whole front of the Isetta opened so the driver and passenger (only one passenger) could get in. I have never seen a car that small and the second car was a Messerschmitt equally unusual. It actually reminded me of the German fighter plane, with the same name. The passenger would sit behind the driver in a cockpit. The top (cockpit) was glass and opened like a airplane's cockpit. I rode in them once and that was enough for me. I don't know what happened to those cars. We took them in large costume crates in the Ice Capades train, from town to town. They were used to get around the cities in which we played. But, I think the skaters felt much safer in a Taxi Cab, and the next year the cars were gone.

People who have seen the shows in the 50's and 60's say the two greatest show skaters ever to headline an ice show were Donna

Atwood and Bobby Specht. Bobby always played a Prince to Donna's Snow White or Cinderella and with Bobby's good looks, he actually looked the part of a Prince. He could have gone to Hollywood a thousand times from offers by Mega Agents Henry Wilson or Dick Clayton; but he just loved skating. Specht once said, "Who knows if I ever took those guys up on their offer and went to Hollywood, I could fall flat on my face and be a flop; but, skating in the show I know I'm not going to fall; So, I'll stay right here thank you and that's what I told them." Naturally there were skaters who could do things that Atwood and Specht couldn't do; but, as Harris always said. "It's not what you do; but, how you do it." and I believe that.

Donna Atwood & Bobby Specht

Joe Jackson Jr., Alan Konrad 'Split Jump', Jackson & Lynam, Comedians

Richard Dwyer

The Old Smoothies, Orrin Markhus & Irma Thomas

The Entire Cast of Peter Pan shot August 1955, on the boardwalk in Atlantic City, for the 1956 show of Ice Capades. (The author of this book second from the right, top row)

A little bit about the choreographers. I don't remember many of them but the ones I do remember stand out. There was Chester Hale, Rod Alexander, John Butler, Rod Alexander, Jose Greco, Donn Arden and last but not least the great Ron Fletcher and his assistant Dick Nord. One day Chester Hale was working on a specialty number with six girls and John H. Harris invited his favorite audience down to watch rehearsals. They were the Roman Catholic Sisters of Mercy about eight of them, one being a Harris cousin, Lucy Mae Harris AKA Sister Mary Dennis. They were we're seated front ice by the dash lights. Harris knew Chester Hale swore like a sailor and asked him to watch his language because of the nuns being in the arena. Well, it didn't do any good at all because Chester screamed out, "Shelia, don't hold your hand like that, you look like you're picking diamonds out of a f--k--g horses ass." The silence in the arena was deafening;

however, the nuns actually thought it was funny, they looked at each other snickering, barely able to control an out and out laugh. Harris flew out on the ice like Peter Pan and again cautioned Hale to watch his mouth. Chester walked over to the nuns and apologized, for his outburst and all was forgiven.. He returned to the girls on the ice and continued working on the number, when all of a sudden the 'F' word filled the arena along with other expletives. Harris was so upset, he walked out on the ice and fired Chester Hale on the spot. The next day however, Hale was back on the job. Chester was probably one of the greatest choreographers who ever lived right along side of movie great Busby Berkeley, Donn Arden, Ron Fletcher and Tony Charmoli. Chester did the show at the Roxey, in New York; and worked in many movies; He choreographed the movie "Anna Karenina" with Greta Garbo and Fredrick March; he danced with the great Anna Pavlova. He even worked with "The Three Stooges" in Reckless. Chester Hale was one of Larry Fine's (Larry from Moe, Curley and Larry) favorite subjects. He actually imitated Chester's swearing, with a New York accent "What the f#ck are you doing?

I told you to get your f#c#ing ass to stage right. Not to stage left,and do it on the third count of four, or can you count that f#c#ing high? " Larry would mess up his hair and he actually looked like Chester Hale as he was impersonating him..

There was another very colorful choreographer with Ice Capades for a short time. He's the choreographer who established the look, of the Las Vegas Showgirls. He's known in Las Vegas as the "The Father of Feathers" we knew him as Donn Arden. Donn set the standard for the Las Vegas Showgirl when he debuted at the Stardust Hotel and Casino in 1959 his show "Lido de Paris" ran until 1991. He directed and choreographed, "Donn Arden's Jubilee" at Bally's; "Hallelujah Hollywood" at the MGM Grand; "Hello Hollywood Hello"at the MGM Grand in Reno.

When Donn decided to become a choreographer he moved to Cleveland, Ohio and went to work for a mobster named Moe Dalitz. Moe owned a few clubs there, with live shows and Donn put the shows together. In time Donn moved on, working with other choreographers and putting numbers together for Broadway shows and then he went to work for

Ice Capades, the movies and with Fred Astire, helping to choreograph his numbers. In the early 50's he moved to Las Vegas and put a show into the Desert Inn Hotel, only to find out that the Hotel that advertised itself as Wilber Clark's Desert Inn Hotel and Country Club, was actually owned by Organized Crime as well as his old employer Moe Dalitz, from the Cleveland Mafia.

Moe was a member of the Purple Gang in Detroit; but when the Feds made things a little too hot for him in Detroit, Moe moved to Cleveland and joined the Mafia Family of Al Polizzi. He later hooked up with Lucky Luciano, The Boss of all Bosses, Head of the Commission, He was the Head of the Five New York Families; The Bannano Family; The Gambino Family; The Columbo Family; The Lucchese Family and the Genovese Family along with Frank Costello, who became hidden owner of The Tropicana Hotel in Las Vegas; Myer Lanski, owned the El Cortez Hotel, the Stardust and the Thunderbird Hotel, in Las Vegas; and Bugsey Segal owned the Flamingo Hotel and El Cortez. But most of the other hotels were already mobbed-up as well.

When Donn Arden was asked by Murray Westgate a television anchorman in Las Vegas about his early career in show business, Donn reluctantly replied, "I hate to use this word; but, I guess I owe my whole career to the Mafia." Donn Arden said, "Moe Dalitz was a good man, he had a lot of money and didn't mind spending it. That's what makes something, especially in show biz, a success".

Ron Fletcher another great choreographer had the same verbal affliction as Chester Hale, only not quite as severe. Ron started out as a Martha Graham dancer. He acted in a couple of movies most notably, "Buck and the Preacher" with Sidney Portier. Ron is truly a man of many talents. One day in Atlantic City Ron was teaching the kids a certain step; but, one of the girls was having a little trouble with it. She was a left foot jumper and this was a right foot problem. Most skaters jump from their left foot but Fletcher, a non skater wanted the kids on the left side of the ice to jump from their left foot and the kids on the right side of the ice to jump from the right foot. Well, Pat Golden was having a little difficulty jumping from her right foot, as were a few others; but, Ron only noticed Pat Golden having problems. So, he let out a barrage of insults and Pat skated off the ice. She came very close to quitting the show when Rosemary Stewart, former Olympic Champion and skating director for Ice Capades told Pat to just ignore Ron's remark, that all choreographers have a short wick and have to be a little crazy to do what they do anyway and tomorrow he probably wouldn't even remember what he said. Rosemary was right the next day Ron bought Pat a coffee and was joking with her backstage and they say elephants can't fly !!!.

Chorographers are kind of like cooks, they all have bad tempers and those who don't, for some reason just don't cut it. Watch Michael Douglas, as the choreographer in "A Chorus Line," The good ones are all like that. What is surprising is that Chester Hale just as did Ron Fletcher, worked with "The Three Stooges." Chester in "Reckless" and Ron in "Snow White and the Three Stooges" Starring Carol Heiss (Jenkins) Edson Stroll and Ice Capet, Pat Huber aka Pat Huber Yeates Ursetta. Ron Fletcher will always be remembered in Ice Capades for his great work in "Peter Pan", "County Fair","Fantasy in Pink","Bolero" and others.

He's truly a one of a kind guy and I'm thrilled to have worked with him.

Jerry Mayhall was hired as the conductor of the orchestra and stayed for 20 plus years. He was a great musician and a well respected member of the show. Bryan McDonald was the MC and Company Manager, he had a voice that could rival Gary Owens of the old T.V. Show, "Laugh-In".

Now who asked where the name Ice Capades came from? The show needed a name just as much as they needed skaters, well, almost. One day a group of guys from the Arena Managers Assn. was sitting around trying to come up with a name for the show. Ice Cycles (a name that was later used, for another show) The World Ice Show, Ice Extravaganza, Ice World, Ice Century and then Boston's Walter Brown said, "Ice Capades #@$%$# I mean Ice Escapades". Harris said, "No, you've said it……..,,. Ice Capades……..That's it….….Ice Capades"……………… So, thanks to a mispronunciation by Walter Brown owner of the Boston Bruins and the Boston Celtics. Now, the greatest show on ice had a name ICE CAPADES…….

Jerry Mayhall Ice Capades Music Director and John H. Harris, Creator, President and Producer

DONNA ATWOOD AND BOBBY SPECHT JOIN ICE CAPADES

In 1942 Donna Atwood joined the show from Newton, Kansas. She was the National Pairs Champion. There was no place for her in the show at that time; but, Rosemary Stewart knew she was star material. Stewart told Harris, "We should hire her, this girl has star possibilities." So, Harris signed her and she was signed as a H.A.P. doing an occasional line number. Every person who ever skated in a professional ice show like Ice Capades, Ice Follies, Disney On Ice or Holiday on Ice knows what H.A.P. means. It means (Half Ass Principle) As an H.A.P. you don't make principle salary; but, you don't make line (chorus) salary either. Within the year Donna was a Principle. Together she starred with Bobby Specht, another National Champion and the greatest team of show skaters was born. Now, they weren't like Torvile and Dean and they couldn't compete with them in structured competition; but, as far as show skating Specht and Atwood were the greatest. They stared in "Snow White", "Cindarella,""Brigadoon,""An American in Paris,""Student Prince,""Wish You Were Here" and Donna Skated in the greatest of all shows, Sir James M. Barry's "Peter Pan" Harris hired the Foys, in England who flew Mary Martin on Broadway, to fly

Donna Atwood. It was a tougher job flying Donna because with Mary Martin the Foys only had to rig the Broadway theater, in which "Peter Pan" was playing. But with Donna and Ice Capades, they had to tear down the rigging and then set it up again, in a new arena, every week or so for 48 weeks. The Foys were the absolute best in their business, no competition. We played 28 arenas that year and each had to be rigged for the flying sequences. It was a monstrous job. Donna would fly 30 to 40 feet in the air, a very dangerous thing to do. But, it never really bothered her, she said Mary Martin did it for all of those years so what do I have to worry about.

Donna Atwood as Peter Pan, Ice Capades of 1956

June Barlow as Tiger Lilly in Peter Pan, in one of the best performances in show and Arthur Clark as the Pirate Smee another great actor and skater.

Actor William Bendex and skater Helen Davidson.

Donna was nothing short of spectacular. I know, because I was there as a skater in the show and I was there every night, I was only a little Indian, but I was an Indian every night skating on the ice with Donna and not a day goes by that something doesn't remind me of "Peter Pan". Donna made John Harris' dreams of producing an ice show, that told a story come true. She was beautiful, She was a great skater and she could act. She was an integral part of John's dreams and an integral part of Ice Capades. Donna could have been one of the screens great actresses; but, she choose ice skating instead and......She was the absolute best!!!

Hans Brinker, Ice Capades '57

An American in Paris, Ice Capades '55

Donna Atwood, An American in Paris

Production Number, Fantasy in Pink

Back in 1943 John Harris was having trouble with his wife. Something wasn't right; but, he didn't know what it was. So he started checking. Now, he had to keep himself busy, so he concentrated on Ice Capades (the Big Show). He hired Orrin Markhus and Irma Thomas, known to the skating world as "The Old Smoothies" Orrin was 51, heavy set and a little sparse on top. Irma was 44, a nice looking woman that all the skaters loved. In many cities, Orrin and Irma stopped the show almost every night. They did nothing more than skate and smile. They were everybody's Mom and Dad. And so many in the audience lived vicariously through "The Old Smoothies" John Harris always said, "It's not what you do; it's how you do it. Just watch "The Old Smoothies."

'The Old Smoothies' Orrin Markhus & Irma Thomas

Also about this time Alan Konrad joined the show. He was a very masculine skater, like Gene Kelly and Gower Champion were dancers. Konrad's jumps were big and high. He was announced as, "The Eagle of the Ice" and that he was. Konrad would do 'slow-mo' open axels, big split jumps and always close his number with three Arabian Cartwheels. He was my favorite male show-skater. There were skaters who did doubles and triples to Konrad's singles and doubles; but, as John Harris would said "It's not what you do, It's how you do it." and Alan Konrad just did it better, than anyone else. His music was even exciting, "Dancing in the Dark," "In The Still of the Night", "Change Partners," all up tempo. Music that would make Sammy Kahn wish he was the composer after watching Alan Konrad skate. Now days, you need a damn laser gun to find out if a jump was a triple or a quad. And frankly Scarlet, I don't give a damn how many revolutions a skater makes. I'd rather watch a good skater do a slow open axel or a split flip, like Alan Konrad or Johnny Littengarver than watch an acrobat with skates do a quad. Now, there are a few exceptions Scotty Hamilton, Kristie Yamaguchi, Michelle Kwan, Tara Lipinski and Kim-Yu-Na, (the 2010 Olympic Champion). I'm sure there are others but those skaters stand out in my mind. But no matter what I'd rather watch Konrad, Dwyer or Littengarver than all the others.

They called him 'The Eagle of the Ice' and that's exactly what Alan Konrad was his jumps were high and long and nobody did it better.

In 1946 John H. Harris along with Roy and Eddie Shipstead and Oscar Johnson from Ice Follies started a third show and called it Ice Cycles. It played smaller cities than the other two shows; but, was very successful. And in just three short years later in 1949 Harris purchased the show outright. He thought that by doing the same show that Ice Capades was doing; but, doing it a year later, it would enable him to use the costumes, for two years rather than one. The same with the sets, the choreography, the music and even the programs, all he would have to do was change the pictures and text.

So, Harris hired the outstanding team of Jamie Lawrence and Margaret Fields, to skate the Donna Atwood and Bobby Specht numbers and BINGO !!! It was another major success. Now, Ice Capades got two years for the price of one. The cast was a little smaller, the cities were not as large, but it didn't seem to matter. The new Ice Cycles went on for seven years, before changing its name to Ice Capades International in 1956. Even some of the acts would switch back and forth, from one show to another. It was a great idea. As a matter of fact, a year later in 1947 "Holiday on Ice" did the same thing. It started "Ice Vogues" to play the smaller cities.

Margaret Field & Jimmy Lawrence, stars of Ice Cycles & Ice Capades Intl.

Jerry Mayhall the orchestra conductor for the Ice Capades used to go to bed shortly after the show and get up early in the morning, which was exactly the opposite from what most of the skaters would do. Jerry was a great guy with a unusual sense of humor; but, like the old saying, 'Don't mess with Texas' you didn't want to mess with Jerry Mayhall. He liked getting up at about 8am, have breakfast at the hotel restaurant and take in the sights of the city we happened to be in. This time it was New Haven. Jerry was having problems with his neighbors in the next room. They were three guys, not with Ice Capades. They were partying and making a lot of noise all night long. After asking them to quiet down numerous times, and to no avail. Jerry got (2) wolfers and (2) tweeters used for rehearsals. They filled the largest arenas with sound. Jerry choose "An American in Paris" to entertain his new friends. He then put the speakers right up against his neighbors wall, turned them up to about 150 decibels and went down stares for breakfast.

The Hotel Manager had to call Jim Harkins the show manager, to shut the speakers off. But Jerry said it only lasted about half an hour. His neighbors moved that day.

There was a skater with Ice Follies who was showmanship unparalleled. His name was Richard Dwyer and he later joined Ice Capades. But, for years he did the same number; but, because of the personality and great talent he put into his act, he was exciting to watch every time. In many cases you knew what Richard Dwyer was going to do next; but, you just wanted to see him do it again. He came out, on the ice, in a black high hat, white tie and tails with six beautiful show-girls, three on each arm. And just before he started his solo, he presented a dozen American Beauty Roses to a woman in the audience, usually an older woman, but not always. Then Richard did his solo, Richard Dwyer was Fred Astire or Gene Kelly definitely the "Debonair on Ice" and he's now in the Hall of Fame. Richard lives in Southern California. Remember his name: Richard Dwyer, he's one of the very best.. When Ice Capades played L.A. I stayed at the Dwyer home in the Hollywood Hills and at that time Richard was also on the road, with Ice Follies.

Next to my own family, if I had to pick the best, most holism and decent family I had ever known, the family I would be honored to call my own would be the Dwyers: Anthony and Mary Dwyer (parents), then Ronald, Richard and Dolores, everyone of them was an exceptional person.

The Debonair of the Ice, Richard Dwyer.

Star of Ice Follies & Ice Capades and a member of the Hall of Fame, one of the very best...

HARRIS GOES HIS OWN WAY

John Harris was now filing for a disillusionment from Lucille. As it happens Lucille was married before; but, neglected to get a divorce. So, she and John were never actually married. Now John was free to do what he wanted. John got custody of John II. John the Dad, started taking Donna Atwood out for lunch; but, only to talk about show business. that's all !!! Then they would go out for dinner once or twice a week; but, only to talk about the show and her numbers, that's all!!! Then Donna started accompanying him on visits, to the homes of the Arena Managers Assn., (stock holders) that wanted to meet her that's all!!!. When the show closed for it's 5 week vacation, Donna either went to John's home in Pittsburgh or to his place in L.A. Finally in 1949, you guessed it, John Harris married his skating Queen. In 1950 she had twin boys Denny and Donny and the following year she had a little girl, they named her Donna Janette but everyone called her Cissy.

Donna, The Twins Denny & Donny and Donna Janette aka Cissy

John H. Harris, Donna, the twins and Cissy

John H. Harris, Donna, the twins and Cissy

I never saw Uncle John so happy, finally had the family he wanted. With one big exception. His adopted son John H. Harris ll. John Sr. and his new family were living in L.A. and John H. Harris ll was in Pittsburgh, with his Aunt and Uncle the Sheridan's, attending school, at Central Catholic High School. John felt that he no longer mattered to his Dad and that he was always the unnecessary 5th wheel on a car. In the years to come John Sr. got him a job with Ice Capades, in marketing with the Marketing Director Jayne Brown; but, that didn't work out. Harris got him a job in Pittsburgh with the Hornets Hockey team; but that didn't work out either. Later Johnny got married, everyone thought that would settle him down and it seemed to for a while. But he had his own problems and he kept them to himself. Our family moved to Scottsdale and Phoenix, Arizona for our Mothers health. So, we weren't in contact with Johnny any longer. He had (5) children, of his own now one of whom, I just became acquainted with again, through a phone call.

Finally, his job came to an end and he got a job on his own, as a taxi driver in Pittsburgh.. And then one night, in 1972 he ended it all, with a .38 cal shot to the head. John H. Harris ll was dead at 38. The family that didn't show Johnny Jr. much love, during his lifetime, didn't show him much love in death either, few attended his funeral, few seemed to care. He's buried in the Harris section in Calvary Cemetery in Pittsburgh.

THE HORNETS 'HIT' MAN

In 1953 the Pittsburgh Hornets were one of the strongest teams in the American Hockey League, Bill Ezinicke was the Hornets bad boy, He had a reputation as the Hornets "hit-man" or "enforcer" as they called him.

This time Bill got a normal 2 minute penalty for slashing. So, as he was sitting in the penalty box a fan in back of the box started calling him filthy names. Then when the names got too much for Bill and he climbed over the glass, still in his skates and uniform. He grabbed a fan by his coat and began to punch him. After about 5 punches the Duquesne Garden ushers managed to pull Bill off the man and Bill was ejected from the game by the head referee.

Two days later Bill is sitting in the office of his lawyer and this is how he explained it with a strong French Canadian accent, "Andeee, when zees man he called me ze ass-hole, this was alright, when he called me ze son of a beeeetch, this was alright too……..Then he called my Mother a name I won't repeat, even to you Andeee and zes was NOT alright. So, I climbed over the glass to keeked his ass".

Well, after hearing Bills explanation Andy had tears in his eyes from laughing. He told Bill he was going before a Judge with six daughters, I believe his name was Hugh O'Boyle and he was going to ask him the same question and instructed Bill to answer it the same exact way. Bill was found guilty of battery and had to pay the man's dental bills, which came to about $5,000.00 and was picked up by the hockey team. Bill had a great personality, his story, personality and accent saved him.

THE ICE CAPADES TRAINING CLASS IN PITTSBURGH

In Pittsburgh we had 12 boys and 12 girls who were trained for the Ice Capades. We learned how to skate properly, we learned routines, how to sell (show biz talk for 'showmanship') and how to skate with a partner. All the things the show expected from it's skaters. These kids in the class didn't get paid but they got a skating pass to skate any time free, a uniform. The girls a blue leotard and a white sweater with Ice Capades on it. The boys got blue pants and the same sweater. The class usually had auditions every 6 months or so. Depending on how many ot the kids got called to the show. Just to get into the class was a big deal, because 9 out of 10 made it to the show. These are some of the kids that made it into a show or Ice Capades in the 50's & 60's:

Margot Snyder, Betty Ingram, Billy Shea, Marty Burke, Donald "Ducky" Falkner, Barbara Shebatka , Janet Adams, Jessie Quatse, Bob Gallagher, Olga Hurenko, Shirley Hannah (Skrak), Jeanie Hollander (Maxfield), Pat Huber (Yeates, Ursetta), Pat Golden (Roman), Evelyn Gray (Shore), Eleanor Sheridan, Harry Sheridan, Denny Sheridan, John Sheridan, Anne Conboy (Hannigan), Bernie Conboy, Pat Clohessy (Wait),

Richie Egan, Jimmy Callahan, Mike Cancel, Sue Gorman (Raymond), Betsy Mader, Judy Ross and Eleanor Baron.

I know I missed a few and I'm very sorry; but, the above mentioned people all made it into a show..........

Bob Gallagher was one of my best friends in those days and right after high school I got a call from Ice Capades. I was to join them at Convention Hall, in Atlantic City, NJ to rehearse for "Peter Pan. But, Gallagher didn't get a call. And as it turned out Alsa MacLaughlan the teacher of the Ice Capades Training Class, in Pittsburgh, told Rosemary Stewart the performance director, of Ice Capades that Bob Gallagher wasn't a strong enough skater. So, my Mother called Uncle John and asked him to hire Gallagher anyway. As it turned out Gallagher joined the show skated well enough, and 40 years later he fooled everyone. He was still there as The Ice Capades Company Manager. Gallagher never knew this story until now.

ICE CAPADES IN ATLANTIC CITY

IT SEEMED LIKE EVERYTHING IN the Harris family was going according to plan. Donna and the kids were happy, spending summers in Atlantic City with the show and living at their fathers home in Longport on the Bay. We always rehearsed the new show in Atlantic City while doing the old show every night. The children would spend hours on John H's boat on the bay, in Longport, with their Mother, Donna Atwood and other members of the cast. John had a big fenced lot, off the side of his home and he would have the cast over for Bar-B-Q and hamburgers, every couple of weeks.

Many times John's friend Larry Fine would join them for the hamburgers. John loved having Larry over, He marveled at how the kids re-acted when they recognizes Larry Fine, but few did, because he didn't look like he did on camera and more than half of the cast didn't recognize him at all. Larry talked to Ice Capet Bernie Conboy for about 20 minutes one day and she never knew who he was. And to top it off, she was a big fan of "The Three Stooges" Larry was one third of "The Three Stooges" Moe, Curley and LARRY. I'll always remember Ice Capet Bernie Conboy as "Flower" the little skunk in the Disney number in Ice Capades. When Bambi asked her what her name was She replied, "You can call me Folwer" and we all did. Bernie Conboy was on of the most beautiful girls in the show, inside and out. She passed away in Pittsburgh and I'll always remember her as a little Angel with skates called Flower and I know she's in Heaven, skating for God's other Angels.

Larry Fine of the "Three Stooges"

Ice Capades Cast at the Harris home in Longport, NJ rehearsing for the new show in Atlantic City. We did the old show at night and rehearse the new show during the day.

Jimmy Grogan, always second in the Olympics and Worlds to Dick Button; but, with the people who knew him he was always number one.

One of the great show skaters Skippy Baxter, the first to do a back flip in his numbers in the 1950's.

A beautiful and exciting skater Sonya Klopfer.

Jenny Baxter as exciting on the ice as Olga Korbit was on the parallel bars; but, with the looks of an Angel.

*Sandy Culbertson another diva that just vaporized.
talented, beautiful and gone…..*

Just about two weeks before we were to leave Atlantic City, with the new show, under our belts, rehearsed and ready to perform in Pittsburgh and New York City. Harris would take the entire cast, including stage hands and musicians to Hackney's Restaurant, for steak or lobster. It was a great time for everyone. I'll never forget those times,............. or the lobster !

THE BRUCE BARRAGE, IN ATLANTIC CITY

HIS NAME WAS BRUCE WILSON and he was one of our skaters. He never tried to hide his being gay. He was very funny and almost everyone liked him. I say almost, because Bruce had a way of irritating the 'Homophobes', in the show, some of the skaters, most of the stage hands and all of the musicians. One night at a big gay club in Atlantic City, I can't remember the name, of the place; but, Bruce was the guest performer. The club announced him as being from Ice Capades and he did a number from "Flower Drum Song" The song was called, "I Enjoy Being a Girl" and was sung by Pat Suzuki, in the movie and Broadway Play "Flower Drum Song". However, Bruce changed the lyrics to be very gay in nature and went something like this: "When I get a brand new hairdo, and a new pair of shoes and bag, I fly through the air like clouds do, I enjoy being a fag." I was there, as were most of the cast members and his performance was harmless. The next day the Company Manager fired him for violating the morals clause in his contract. Well, don't feel sorry for Bruce. Here is how he got back into the Ice Capades. There was a bar across from the Convention Hall called Nick Talley's. So, they put a big banner out in front of the bar, that couldn't be missed by people going into the arena to see Ice Capades. The sign said "BRUCE WILSON former star of Ice Capades appearing nightly: shows at......8.....10....and midnight. John Harris was just furious when he saw the banner. He stormed over across the street to the bar and told Bruce to "Get that God Damn sign down and be back at work tomorrow." Bruce was back the next night. And the kids were just thrilled because Bruce kept the kids laughing.

Nick Tally loved the kids in the show, because they spent a lot of time and bucks at his bar, but not just because of that. They were never any trouble; so, you can bet he was in on the whole thing, with Bruce Wilson. Nick Tally had some really great jazz music. Slam Stewart played his base there for a couple of weeks, Wes Montgomery, Milt Buckner and J. J. Johnson and many more would all sit in when they were in town.

There was also another bar on the Boardwalk, just north of the Convention Hall we used to call it "The Church" As I understand it, a few guys were late a few of times, for rehearsals and Harris said to them, "Why the hell are you guys always late?" and one of the guys knowing Harris was a religious man replied, "We were at church Mr. Harris" That was enough for Harris, he said, " OK; but, find an earlier Mass next time" and walked away. So, it became known as 'The Church'. I can't even remember the real name of the place. However, and you're not going to believe this, It just recently happened, one of the former Ice Capets, Nan Horner e-mailed me with the real name of that bar, it was The Auditorium Lounge. It's amazing but for 20 years I couldn't think of the real name of The Church and neither could anyone else. Everybody I ever asked called it the Church and they didn't know the real name either. Thanks a million Nan !!!

Convention Hall, Atlantic City, Our home away from home. It will always be remembered as the home of 'Ice Capades' and 'The Miss America Pagent'

Ice Capet Patty Davis Gur

Ginny Iverson Jones from England

ON THE BOARDWALK - IN ATLANTIC CITY

THERE WERE THOUSANDS OF THINGS to do in Atlantic City, in the 50's and 60's take a walk down the Boardwalk, or ride in a Rolling Chair, pushed by a man. You could go to the Steeplechase Pier, a great place for kids, big and little. It had Amusement rides of all descriptions. You could spend the day there and wonder where the time went. The Steeplechase Pier was right next to the larger Steel Pier, which was (1000 feet out in the Atlantic Ocean). There you could watch a horse actually dive into the Atlantic Ocean, or hear Woody Herman and The Third Heard or Stan Kenton and his Orchestra play in the Ball Room or even see, "West Side Story" at one of the two Steel Pier Theaters. There were many small stores along the boardwalk you could see a demo-man much like Billy May demonstrate the glass knife that never needs sharpening and could cut through a beer can, well, that's what they told the people anyway. There was that Salt Water Taffy machine, in the Fralinger's Salt Water Taffy store that made that wonderful Salt Water Taffy from Atlantic City. Salt Water Taffy that was sent all over the world from Fralinger's in Atlantic City. Riding down the wooden Boardwalk in one of those Rolling Chairs and they have been doing that since the 1800's, you could see a little bit of everything. The woman walking down the Boardwalk, in 90 degree heat, in a fur coat and sun glasses. The happy Mother and Father with their three little boys, all dressed in sailor suits, with excitement stamped all over their little faces and with a large lollypop in their hands. Day or night you could smell the aroma of peanuts, from the Planters Peanut Store. On the way back to the Convention Hall, there was The Pizza Store with 10 cent slices, right next to the High End Fur Salon. There were the Grand old hotels of yesteryear on the right, The Traymor, The Dennis, The Marlborough-Blenheim, The Sherbourne and The Claridge. Not far away was Hackney's and Captain Stern's Seafood Restaurants, the two best in Atlantic City in the 50's. And just up the street was Skinny D'Amato's "500 Club" where Frank Sinatra and Martin & Lewis played. Those were the days. I remember seeing Jerry Lewis shortly after the break up with Dean Martin. Jerry ended his show by singing, "I'll Go my Way by Myself" Well, I'll tell you this, I wish I had the Kleenex concession after that number.

THE ICE CAPADES PERFORMERS GROUP AND THE 'KIDS'

Now days there is an organization called 'Ice Capades Performers Group'. Started by former Ice Cadet P.J. Ramano, now a stand-up comedian, with the help and assistance of former Ice Cadet Ken Shook, who now works for FOX-Atlanta, Both of the guys are still in the Biz....

Ice Capades Performers Group is on the internet and many of the kids who were in the show as skaters, stage hands or musicians are members and keep in contact with each other that way. It's a great idea, I haven't talked with some of the kids for more than 30 plus years and because of this group, were in contact again. It's funny, that no matter how old you are, you're always refered to as kids.

You might be 75 years old now; but, to the gypsies you're still a kid. Gypsy is another name for Kid !!! This 'kid' business, is not just limited to ice skaters. Broadway has it's kids and the traveling shows such as "Chorus Line" and River Dance have their kids, all of the shows use the same nomenclature......................This kid joined Ice Capades Training Class in Pittsburgh, when I was 15 years old and skated with the class until I was 17 and graduated from high school. I was called into the big show (Ice

Capades) and believe it or not, I haven't seen or talked to some of those kids since I left the class for the show. But, because of the Ice Capades Performers Group were old pals again. There are reunions every ten years; but, recently changed to every five years. I think because of some of our ages. The reunions are headed up by Gloria Lor Spoden, Ken Shook and Stephan Kolvan. However, there are mini re-unions every year or so, in cities around the U.S.A. and Canada. This re-union business is a great idea to keep the Ice Capades family together, because like the Marines, "Once an Ice Capet or Ice Cadet always an Ice Capet or Ice Cadet."

ICE CAPADES-ON THE ROAD

W E ALWAYS TOOK THE ICE Capades train to our next city. The train had freight cars for the sets, the Zamboni and the costumes as well as (1) girls cars, (1) boys cars, and a married couples car. We used to turn one of the men's lounges into a card room, and fill the sink up with ice and beer on almost Every trip and have a little poker game. One night I was just watching and I noticed Irma Thomas, one of the Old Smoothies throw away a winning hand. She had a full house and the "winner" had a low three of a kind. I said , "Irma you tossed away a winning hand. "She looked at me and said very quietly, "I know what I'm doing just be quiet." The next morning at breakfast, on the train she told me she won a couple of big pots, on the last train trip and she felt terrible, because she won the money from a line boy (chorus boy), who needed it much more than she did. And he was the one that got the money when she threw in the winning hand. "That's why I did it" she said, "I'd feel better if you just keep that to your self." Well, I kept that to myself until now. And since Irma has gone to heaven to be with Orrin, I guess it's OK to talk about it now. Orrin and Irma lived in Palm Springs, CA and loved it down there Orrin was crazy about old cars and had a collection of them. Orrin and Irma were two of a kind.......two of the Best!!!

This is what we did on our train trips....Guess !!!
Eric Wait, unknown, Jimmy Grogan, unknown, unknown,
Freddie Trenkler.

Our guys having an adult beverage, on the train before arriving at our next city. L to R Phil Romayne, unknown Freddie Trenkler, Bobby Specht, unknown.

There were so many great people and outstanding skaters in the show I feel bad that I'm going to overlook most of them. But here goes anyway, Nate and Edith Walley; Nate was a one time company manager and principle skater and skating coach. He even created the 'Walley Jump'. Edith was also a principle skater who later became the shows costume mistress. I'll never forget the time Nate (the Principle skating coach) challenged Ronnie Robertson (Olympic Champ) to a spinning contest. Now, Nate was in his 50's and Ronnie at 18, had just won silver in the Olympics. The rules were laid down and agreed to by both parties. It wasn't to be who could spin the fastest; but, who could spin the longest. There was no question that

Ronnie Robertson was the fastest spinner in the world. So, there was no contest there.

Now the contest begins: Bobby Specht (A National Champ Himself) timed the event, with his stop watch. Ronnie immediately goes into his famous 'Blur Spin' and Nate goes into a slow cross foot spin. Minutes go by and because of the energy Ronnie has been putting into his spins you could see his energy was depleting, but Ole Nate was spinning like a top. Now, Nate decided to go into a sit-spin and get a little rest. Ronnie notices the change and goes into a camel spin, costing him more energy. Anyway, Ronnie finally quit, he stepped over the dash and took off his skates.

Nate was still spinning and Ronnie just shook his head. Nate finally quit; but, he could have gone on for much more time. "There is a moral to this little competition" said Nate, "Much like the two bulls who spot a heard of cows grazing about half a mile away. The young bull said lets RUN down there and have our way with one of those cows. The old bull says no..........Lets WALK down there and have our way with them all". Nate looked at Ronnie and said "Ya see Ronnie, in this case, you were the young bull."

The Walley's daughter, Deborah Walley replaced Sandra Dee as Gidget, in the movie "Gidget goes Hawaiian" 1961. She also starred with Elvis Presley in, "Spinout" in 1966 and many others. She had a brother sister relationship with Elvis Presley and remained good friends until his death. She stayed active in theater running a small theater in Sedona, Arizona until her death, in 2001 from esophageal cancer.

Jimmy Grogan as far as people go, was the best. He was a National Champion, always coming in second to Dick Button. He was a World Class Skater and a World Class Guy. He loved his Irish heritage and was respected by every member of the cast and crew. Jimmy liked to hang out with his wife, stage hands and chorus kids, because he said they were his type of people. (Jimmy's words)

Jimmy Grogan

There was Patty and John Curtain a great adagio team. They looked so good on the ice, they didn't have to do a damn thing; but, they could...................and the audience loved them.

One of the best, if not the very best was Phil Romayne and Terry Brent later Cathy Steele. When I think of professional pair skaters they're the first ones that come to my mind.

Ronnie Robertson, Lynn Finnigan, Cathy Steele, Phil Romayne

Herb Cowman could do everything, he did the play-by-play announcing for the badminton team, almost as well Steve Savard does for the St. Louis Rams Football Team, I said almost !!!. Herb was Captain Hook, in Peter Pan and was a marvelous skater and a superb actor. There wasn't a damn thing that Herbie couldn't do in show biz. There was Willie Kall a Pittsburgher who joined the show as a line skater and in no time he was a star. Willie was a comedian and in one of his numbers he dressed up as a ballerina and surprised everyone, when he started to trip and slip and slide the audience caught on and loved his act. Walt Disney loved it so much he asked Harris to allow Willie to do his act on the "Mickey Mouse Club" national television show and he did.

In Ice Capades, in those days, acting was a big part of the shows success. Donna as Peter Pan, Rosemary Henderson as Wendy and June Barlow as Tiger Lilly, Herbie Cowman as Captain Hook and Arthur Clark as Smee, they were all convincing and wonderful actors as well as great skaters. I should point out that June Barlow never received the recognition she deserved. She was absolutely outstanding as Tiger Lilly and I never think of Peter Pan without thinking of June Barlow as Tiger Lilly. I don't know of anyone who could have done it better.

I have to mention a few other skaters, some were principles some were in the line kids ; but, all indispensable to the success of the show. Pat Matthews, the line captain, was a beautiful girl from Australia. Her responsibilities were to run heard over the line, making sure the girls kicks, in the kick line were high enough and at the same height and that the line was straight. She was also in charge of the weigh-ins which we had every week, in reality she was the Shows First Sergeant.

The girls really hated weigh-ins, because for some reason their weight fluctuated more that the guys. One day the assistant line captain, was doing the weigh-ins and one of the chorus girls from Scotland, who knew she was going to be over her weight limit said, "I don't feel very well and I'm having my period now." The assistant line captain looked at her sympathetically and said, "Well dearie, how much does your Tampex weigh?"

Bill Dougherty was the men's line captain. Did you ever know a person who you just couldn't swear in front of, because he reminded you of a priest or pastor? Well, Bill was that kind of guy. However, if you weren't doing your job he would come after you. Nobody has heard from Bill Dougherty since he left the show or they're not talking. We always called him Father Bill and maybe, just maybe he got himself ordained somewhere. Henry Seguin always knew the best places to eat, in almost every city we played in and he always had the directions to "Party Central". If you ever wanted to know where the best Steak House was, you asked Henry. He had that special gift of humor and kindness, which modestly packaged, describes Henry Seguin. There are just a few skaters I have to mention, for their personality, humor even loyalty and they are: Ginny Iverson, a beautiful girl from England, with a sense of humor to match; Lee and Sylvia Brink honest and true friends and special friends of Donna Atwood ; Richie Eagan, a family friend from Pittsburgh, Richie went from skater to wardrobe director at CBS to' Hawaii-50' a life long friend ; Dick Ekstrom, a good friend; Jimmy Callaghan always celebrating St. Patrick's Day; Jean Alsop who joined the show from England; Bill Marshall and Jack Vanderware, talented skaters as well as great guys; Marilyn Holt, everyone's sister; Christian Morreau, who joined the show from France; and of course my pal and long time friend Claudia Lattin. I know I've missed hundreds of names and I truly sorry.

A few of us were having some adult beverages one night and on our way home the driver who shouldn't have been driving in his condition, turned left and stayed in the left lane when of all things an Atlantic City Policeman stepped out in front of the car motioning for us to stop. Bob stopped the car and we all got out. The policeman was irate, "What the hell are you guys doing, going down the wrong side of the street?" At that point Marty Ryan, a principle from Australia just took over. "He said "Sir, were with Ice Capades and the boys were celebrating, maybe a little too much and I was driving them home. But I'm not quite used to driving here in the states, being from Australia and for a few seconds I thought I was in the correct lane. That is until I saw you." The cop gave Marty a little lecture about driving in America, slapped him on the back and left the scene, never realizing that Marty wasn't the driver, in the first place. His name was Bob Gallagher and he was under the weather.

Bobby Specht (not the driver of the car) should have been a P.R. guy. He had the best personality God was giving out the year he was born. Bobby was also a great skater a National Champion. He was a mixture of a ballet dancer and a Gene Kelly. He skated solos and with Donna Atwood. In 'Student Prince', 'An American in Paris' and 'Brigadoon' no one was better. And nobody looked more like a Prince than Bobby Specht. I have to mention that "An American in Paris" was one of the most spectacular numbers I have ever witnessed. Bobby Specht and Donna Atwood WERE Gene Kelly and Cyd Cherres, that's how good they were. Just like the movie, it's as though movie director Vincente Minnelli directed the show and Gene Kelly choreographed it. The music was astounding and penetrating. I almost put Jerry Mayhall in the same class as Bill Conti from "Rocky"…..I said almost!!! Not only did I watch, "An American in Parris" time and time again, I loved the music and chorography; but, one night Rosemary Stewart, the Performance Director said, "Tomorrow morning I want you to learn Mike Flaherty's Gendarme number in "An American in Paris" and be ready to do it the next night" I told her I was learning my numbers in "Peter Pan" and she said, "We need you to do it….Why, because the costume fits you". So, not only did I love 'An American in Paris'; but, I ended up in it.

Frank Zamboni, who invented the ice re-surfacer was from Paramount, California and sold Ice Capades the second Zamboni Ice Resurfacing Machine ever made. We took it with us, from city to city. it was almost like having another act in the show. When it drove out on the ice, for the first time, people were amazed and many of them stayed in their seats and watched the Zamboni do its magic, right through the intermission. The audience was used to seeing (4) men scraping the ice with snow type shovels. Then a jeep would come out pulling a giant ice scraper with a blade attached. Then when the ice was shaved, the four men would come back out pushing (4) 55 gal drums, on wheels filled with water and running through a 4 foot sponge/brush type instrument for wetting the ice. This method took about (5) times as long and required (5) men. Now, every arena owns a Zamboni or a copy of one.

When Ice Capades played Russia, the audiences were also intrigued with the Zamboni and when the show was getting ready to leave and return to the United States, the Russian police impounded the Zamboni for some phony reason and six months later they had their own Zambomi................. The Ice Capades kids called it "The Olga Zamboni"!!! As it turned out, they just wanted to copy ours; so, they could make their own.

In 1961 the Ice Capades trip to Russia was the world's most successful tour, for any traveling show.

ICE CAPADES AND THE TOAST OF THE TOWN

SO, AFTER REHEARSALS, FOR THE new show in Atlantic City, we went to Pittsburgh and opened there, at the Duquesne Gardens. Playing in Pittsburgh was something special, because Ice Capades was conceived in Pittsburgh in1940 during a Pittsburgh Hornet's hockey game with Sonja Henie skating during the two periods. And it's founder John Harris watching Sonja and dreaming of an ice show that would tell a story like Peter Pan, Snow White, Cinderella and offering more than just an ice show and become The Greatest Show On Ice and known the world over as Ice Capades…Ice Capades had an early rehearsals in New Orleans to try out acts, numbers and personnel and its final dress rehearsal, a sort of Mini Premier in Hershey, PA.(Ice Capades honorary Home Town)

I was born in Pittsburgh and I loved skating there, especially at the Duquesne Gardens. I lived at home, when we played Pittsburgh. I could spent time with my brothers and sister. Next we were off to New York City and to Madison Square Garden, Probably the most famous arena in the world. And while there, we were to appear on CBS-TV's "The Toast of the Town" Better known as "The Ed Sullivan Show" My Mother was in New

York to see us on The Ed Sullivan Show". And to watch Donna, her sister-in-law, do "Peter Pan". She was in the lighting booth with her brother John Harris and asked John, "Which one is Johnny (Me)" Just as she said it, I swear I skated over a hair pin or something and hit the ice, sliding right into the dash lights. John Harris replied, "There he goes now, sliding across the ice, into the dash lights. I think he's just trying to get your attention"

Believe it or not I got fan mail addressed to: The Boy Who Fell on The Ed Sullivan Show % Ice Capades, Madison Sq. Garden, NYC, NY. I say fan mail....It was (3) letters, (2) from old ladies, who thought I got hurt..

THE GREAT HUNTING CAPER

HERSHEY WAS A BEAUTIFUL LITTLE town. Most of the skaters stayed at the The Community Inn. It was just a short walk to the Arena, through a inspiring little park, past a small lake filled with swimming ducks and Canadian Geese, flaping their wings. It was this that attracted the attention of passers by and sparked the epicurean fantasies of three of the English skaters, from the show. These guys decided to do a little illegal hunting, duck hunting. I'm sure without benefit of N.R.A. membership Tony Swift and my good English friend Arthur Clark both principle skaters and Inkey who, worked for the Foys as a flyer, for Donna (Peter Pan). went to the local 5 &10 store and bought a bow and arrow. They all roomed together and decided to have roast duck on the menu, for the next nights dinner. The very next afternoon they went to the park, with their bow and arrows and a string tied around one of their arrows, to pull in their prize kill. They picked out their duck and shot it and after a couple more tries, the great white hunters shot number two. Well, at the Hershey Arena, right after the overature the Pennsylvania State Police arrived back stage, looking for the three Englishmen, who were hunting on state property, out of season, without a hunting license. They had five or six charges against each of the guys. The police decided to let them finish the show, before booking them. Fortunately John Harris was in town and few knew it; but, he graduated from Georgetown University Law School and was a Pennsylvania lawyer. He never practiced; but, was a member of the bar. Harris posted the bond for the "Hunters" who were lucky Harris was there at all, because they would have been put in jail if he wasn't. I'm sure the three learned, it was a fowl thing they did that night.

THE LAMBRETTA RACE

We did a number called Autorama, in the show. The girls dressed like little sexy Cadillacs and the guys dresses like cops.

The guys were riding on Lambretta motor scooters. When the bosses weren't around we had a lot of fun with the Lambretta motor scooters. We would race around the arena with our scooters. I wasn't the best driver; but, for some reason my Lambretta was faster than the others and I always came in 1st or 2nd. One day we were racing around Madison Square Garden, in New York and the guy behind me, Jesse Quatse was yelling something. I couldn't hear him and he wasn't looking where he was going. And #$@*%$$#@# "BANG" he crashed into a telephone booth, in the lobby. It was the loudest noise I think I ever heard. Fortunately he wasn't hurt, Jesse Quatse was a big tough guy from Pittsburgh a Varsity Football Player for Carnegie Tech now Carnegie Mellon University. Not the type of guy you would expect to find, in the line of Ice Capades; but, there were a few big guys like Jesse in the show. The fender of the Lambretta looked like a bent shoe horn. Thank goodness one of our stage hands George Frye was in the building. He took the fender off straightened it out with a rubber hammer and even spray painted it. He borrowed a hair dryer from the girls dressing room and dried the paint. You couldn't even tell it was wrecked. George was like a (D.I.) Drill Instructor in the Marines. He was always yelling at people; but, deep inside his heart was as soft as mashed potatoes. And at 6' 3" and 275 pounds. George ate a lot of mashed potatoes.

It seems that every show one or two of the scooters would slip and fall on the ice and sometimes the skater riding it would get hurt, not seriously but he would hurt his leg and be off for a day or so. Then one day we were addressing the Lambretta problem and Mel Daugherty, one of the skaters who was always joking around. Said, "Mr. Harris why don't you leave some of the air out of the tires?" Harris responded with, "Mel I pay you to skate not to think." That was in 1955 and I don't think anybody has forgotten about it yet. They talked about putting cleats on the tires, putting chains on the tires, but that would have damaged the ice, for the next acts. When Harris said, to one of the stage hands, "Chuckie try leaving some of the air out of the tires." Well, that did it. The scooters hardly ever fell after that. The kids in the show even the stage hands started calling Mel Daugherty, " Mr. Lambretta."

In Boston, during a rehearsal, we got our Christmas Bonuses, which by todays standards would be kind of meager. But all of us principles included got $100.00 which at that time, in the 50's, was pretty generous. Bobby Specht the main male skater got his envelope, took out the $100.00 bill and put it in his dance belt. (A dance belt holds you in like a jock strap; but, supports your back as well.) Well, Bobby returned to rehearsal and after a time he had to go to the men's room. He did his business, flushed the toilet and stood up, just in time to see the $100.00 bill, in a whirl pool going down the toilet drain. Hearing him tell the story was just hilarious.

I'm not sure if I should mention this but it happened; so, I will. It was also in Boston a very sad thing occurred at the Manger Hotel. Our room was on the 6th floor and my roommate, at the time Reg Phillips was writing home to his parents in Hamilton, Ontario, Canada. The desk was positioned next to and facing the window. When he looked up, he saw Ray Curell go by the window from the floor above. Reg yelled and woke me up. He told me what he saw. I looked out the window and sure enough, there was a person lying down below, on the 2nd floor roof. As it turned out, one of our stage hands Ray Curell had a big argument with his wife, who rarely traveled with him. Ray decided to end it all and dove through the bedroom window . I don't know the whole story, I just know everyone was affected by what Ray did. He was very well liked and was an important part of the show. We all missed him. The skaters were really a family and each of us was effected by the loss of Ray.

The Ice Capades programs, were a great memento of the show, not just for the public; but, for the cast as well. It has pictures, names and an itinerary of the places we've been, as well as the dates. We learned how important this was, when we tried to figure out where we were in December of a certain year. The work that went into putting the programs together was mind boggling. Choosing the colors, the type of paper, the photographers and show numbers to be featured in the program. However, the big job was choosing an illustrator to do the coversand Ice Capades had two of the best: Joe DeMers and George Petty.

Joe DeMers: was known in the 40's for his sexy pin-ups. He later attained fame as an illustrator for the Saturday Evening Post. Between 1927 and 1937, DeMers worked for Warner Brothers in the art department. In 1946 DeMers got the biggest break of his life time, painting the girls in Esquires "Gallery of Glamor" and in 1953 his pin-ups gained a new audience, a family audience when he did the program cover for the Ice Capades program. DeMers said he received more notoriety, for doing the Ice Capades program, than anything else he ever did.

George Petty was another illustrator, The Petty's girls were everywhere, even in the movies. In 1950 Robert Cummings, Joan Caulfield and Elsa Lanchester starred in the movie, "The Petty Girls" A motion picture about George and his beautiful girls. Tippi Hedren, star of the "Birds" was a little more than an extra in that movie. For seven years George Petty did the art work, for the cover of the Ice Capades program. They were life like and beautiful. I remember everyone of them. George's girls were featured in advertisements for Jantzen bathing suits, Old Gold Cigarettes, Esquire Magazine, Pepsi Cola and Marshall Fields, in Chicago. For ten years George had the tough job, as one of the judges, in the Miss America Pagent, in Atlantic City. Somebody once said, "When you touch the wrist of a Petty Girl, you almost expect to feel a pulse." Try it….It's true!!!

But beauty didn't stop George's girls from being fined for doing something against the company rules, like sitting in their costumes, smoking or eating in costume etc. The costumes were in some cases as much as $2,500.00 each. They had mirrors and bugle beads, sequences and ever white fox (and that was 1955 money).

And some of the girl's hoop skirts even lit up. You had to be very careful in those costumes because they had to last two years. Ice Capades Inc. did a show one year and Ice Capades International (formerly Ice Cycles) did the same show a second year. So, each show lasted two years. Ice Capades International played smaller cities like Johnstown, Tucson, Spokane, Little Rock, El Paso, Reno while Ice Capades Inc. played larger cities like Pittsburgh, New York City, Cleveland, Boston, Chicago. Dallas, Los Angeles and Saint Louis etc.

In the 50's and 60's almost everybody smoked and I'm talking about Olympic and World Champions. It wasn't until the mid 60's that the medical community pinned all the cancer cases, heart problems and emphysema on smoking. Helen Davidson and Donna Atwood used to do Camel commercials but Donna smoked L&M. I hate to admit she smoked at all; but, in those days we just didn't know how dangerous smoking was.

Donna Atwood doing a Camel Cigarette commercial.

Ice Capades Inc. the big show as it was called, only played two cities in Canada, Toronto and Montreal. One thing about traveling to Canada was the fact that we could only bring one carton of cigarettes per person. However, we were there for almost four weeks. So, all of the kids who didn't smoke took cigarettes for those who did. But, it was still not enough, for the smokers. So, we smuggled them across the border. How did we do it you ask??? Well, we had (2) large kettle drums and (1) large base drum in the orchestra. So, the drummer, Bill Dennis, wrote the names of the owners on the carton of cigarettes, took the heads off the drums and filled them up with the cigarettes.

THE "FINE" PARTY

We would have a 'Fine' party every year paid for by the money collected by the fines imposed on the kids for messing up. What they did was put the money into a bank and around Christmas time, when we were in Boston, at the Manger Hotel, we had a great party. The bosses were always there so everyone was well behaved. But, all the kids usually had a great time. The Hotel was right above the Boston Gardens; So, what many of us would do, was to put our makeup on, in our rooms, put on a robe (the show gave everyone terrycloth robes, that we wore back stage) and we would hop onto an elevator, go down to the back stage of the Boston Gardens. It was a great deal, no cabs, no travel, it was just from your room, to the elevator, to the dressing room in the Boston Gardens. Most all of the kids just loved playing Boston.

There was a place we played in Springfield, Massachusetts we called Eddie Shore's Igloo, because hockey Hall of Fame member, the great Eddie Shore owned it. However, it was always about 10 degrees colder than a well diggers butt; but, when we thawed out it was a great place.

In Philadelphia, we played the old Arena. It had a lot of history; but, it was really a dump in 1955. It was right next to the television station where Dick Clark was doing "American Bandstand" show. In the afternoons you could see the kids standing outside waiting to get into the studio. Some of the kids were so well known, from doing the show you could recognize them standing outside. Most of our kids stayed at the Walnut Park Plaza and right across the street from the arena we caught the "El" to the hotel. That was pretty nice. The "El" was like a subway on stilts. The train was above ground.

In Toronto, we played the famous Maple Leaf Gardens, a great arena with a lot of history. It was almost the Madison Square Garden of Canada, one of the great Arenas. It was just a short walk to our hotel down Jarvis Street. We didn't know it at that time; but, the street, Jarvis St. was where the Ladies of the Evening congregated. So, a few of the guys got to know the ladies on a first name basis. However, there is great beauty and history in Toronto and most of us loved the town.

Another great arena Ice Capades played in was "The Forum" in Montreal, Canada home of one of the worlds great hockey teams, the Montreal Canadians. In one of the worlds most beautiful cities, with great night clubs, elegant restaurants and horse drawn carriages outside the hotels, surrounded by picturesque mountains. It's just a beautiful and exciting city.

We opened the new Coliseum in Charlotte, in 1956 and almost everyone liked that town, the coliseum and the people.

I think if you took a vote in the 50's and 60's, with the skaters the five most popular places we played would have been:

#1 Pan Pacific Auditorium in Los Angeles.
#2 The Convention Hall in Atlantic City
#3 Madison Square Garden, in New York.
#4 The Forum, in Montreal Canada,
#5 Boston Gardens, Boston, MA

Michael Carrington, The British Champion and I were tied for the most fines the first year.

After the 'fine' people would come up to me and Michael and thank us for the party. I have to tell you about Michael Carrington though. Michael did a double axel in his number almost every night (A double axel is jumping from a front outside edge into the air and making two and a half revolutions in the air and landing on a back outside edge.) This was a very difficult jump in those days and it still is. Anyway, Michael would make bets through another person, betting wether he would fall or not. If $80.00 was bet that he was going to fall and $20 was bet that he wouldn't fall. He wouldn't fall and he'd clear $60.00 minus 30% for the guy making the bets. (I promised not to mention his name) The fact is Michael could make the double axel every day like clockwork. Had any of the show's management known this, that would have been the end of Michael's skating days.

So many funny things happened in Boston. One Sunday morning I was going to mass, Church was right across the street, from the hotel. In the lobby of the hotel I saw Rosie Henderson she was about the cutest girl in the show and the Canadian Champion. I asked her where she was going and she said ,"I'm going to Mass" I said "Me too" So she said," lets go or we'll be late." The Mass took forever and ever and the priest was as boring as a rap singer trying to sing the classics. Finally we just had to go or we'd be late for check in (another infraction you can be fined for) As Rosie and I were walking out of the church the priest said very loudly, "People the Mass isn't over yet." Little Rosie, whose as quiet as a church mouse most of the time, stopped in her tracks, spun around like she was in a blur spin and said……..

"It's over for us Father, We have a matinee to do." On our way out I said, "Rosie, what do you think those people thought, when you said we have a matinee to do? They don't know were in Ice Capades at Gardens". Rosie said, "Who cares, next Sunday we'll be in Providence." I mentioned that to Rosie at the most recent Ice Capades re-union party in Las Vegas in 2010 and she said, "How did you remember that?"……..

Rosemary Henderson, one of the very best, as an actress in Peter Pan, a pair skater with Bobby Maxon and a soloist, a beautiful skater and a true Champion.

THE GREAT CROCODILE CAPER

In "Peter Pan" there was an Crocodile that was a part of the story. It was a motorized version (on batteries) operated by a skater named Lyall Stevenson. Anyway, Lyle got into an argument with a couple of the Pirates and for a few weeks they just didn't get along. These guys thought they would give Lyle the business. So they went out to a trick store, in downtown Boston and bought one of those fake "turds". They put the fake "turd" into the crocodile along with a hardy helping of Limberger Cheese. It was terrible and smelled like the real thing. The Crocodile made its entrance on stage left and I made my entrance on stage right, about 60 feet away and even at that distance the smell was permeating. Some of the guys went into the boys dressing room to get their after shave. They poured it into the crocodile so Lyle could crawl into it and do his number. When John Harris heard about it, Lyall was called into the office and asked what he knew about it. But Lyall being the pro he was, said he didn't have any idea who would do such a thing. He said he had no enemies in the show and just couldn't figure it out. Harris thought that one of the local stage hands may have done it and asked our stage hands (those stage hands that travel with the show) to keep an eye on the local guys. I think everybody in the show really knew who did it; but, no one was talking. It was one of those things that was funny to talk about; but, in reality wasn't much of a joke. It could have sabotaged the Crocodiles entrance and ruined that part of the show. I know Donna Atwood (Peter Pan) knew who did it; but, she just kept her little secret.

Donna Atwood, Peter Pan; Rosemary Henderson, Wendy; Herb Cowman, Capt. Hook; June Barlow, Tiger Lilly.

AUTORAMA Cast

THE ICE CAPADES IN LOS ANGELES

PLAYING LOS ANGELES WAS ALMOST like a Motion Picture Premier it's not like that today. Probably because most of the stars don't live in Los Angeles anymore. But, in the 50's and 60's every star in town came to the Ice Capades, including Army Archer the T.V. and newspaper columnist, George Putnam and Jerry Dunphy the television news anchors. And then at intermission many of the stars would come back stage. I remember ending a number and right in front of me was the most beautiful woman I had ever seen. She was so close I could actually touch her. Her name was Rhonda Flemming and beside her was Jeannie Crain, both "11's". That night I remember seeing Robert Taylor, Judy Garland, Peri Angeli, Tab Hunter, Mickey Rooney, Walter Pidgeon, Lex Barker, Charles Colburn and his wife Elsa Lanchester, Clark Gable, Debbie Reynolds and Eddie Fisher, Janet Leigh and Tony Curtis, Robert Wagner, Dewey Martin, Caesar Romaro, Elizabeth Taylor, Michael O'Shea and more. And most of them came backstage during intermission. People would line up for half a day just to get into Ice Capades on Premier Night.

Crowds waiting to get into the box office for opening night tickets

Comedian Willie Kall, with President and Nancy Reagan then Governor of California.

Freddie Trenkler, Sonja Henie and Ronnie Robertson, three of the greatest.

Robert Wagner with Arthur Clark in the background.

Donna Atwood with Dick Powell and June Allison.

Walter Pidgeon and Donna Atwood.

Donna Atwood with Clark Gable and Anita Colby.

Donna and Elizabeth Taylor

Pan Pacific Auditorium was the arena we skated in, when we were in Los Angeles. We would do picture calls for the next years show while there. So, most of the kids were ready to take a little time off. We had four or five weeks off before we started it all over again, in Atlantic City. Olympic Silver Medalist Ronnie Robertson had recently joined the show as did the lovely Cathy Machado, another Olympic Champion. Ronnie had just won the free style skating portion of the Olympics and received a silver medal. In those days Figure Skating was divided into two parts: figures and free skating with figures counting for more points. So, David Jenkins did better in figures and won gold, Even though Ronnie Robertson was a better free skater and would win the Olympics, if both competed today.

Tab Hunter. a friend of Ronnie Robertson and a big movie star in the 50's, 60's and '70's was a great ice skater himself and could have easily skated in the show. Tab would come down to watch rehearsals and a funny thing happened involving Tab. He arrived at the Pan Pacific Auditorium in his new car a Mercedes Benz 300 SL with Butterfly doors and 5 forwards. Well Tab drove all the way, from the San Fernando Valley to the arena in 1st and 2nd gear because he didn't know how to shift a car with 5 forwards. And he didn't want to tell the salesman that he didn't know how to drive it. So, Ronnie Robertson and Henry Seguin went out to give Tab some driving lessons.

HANS BRINKER AND THE SILVER SKATES

Ice Capades was doing "Hans Brinkes and the Silver Skates" in 1957, it was the show of 1958 and it was a Great Show; but, not as popular as "Cinderella",

"Hans Brinker". Donna Atwood had retired after "Peter Pan" and the new star was Rosemary Henderson with the perennial star Bobby Specht.

"Snow White" or "Peter Pan" because the children didn't know the story. We appeared on the "Toast of the Town" again, better known as "The Ed Sullivan Show". I stayed at the St. Moritz Hotel on Central Park South, between the Essex House and The Saint Regis Hotel. They gave the skaters a special rate. But most of the kids didn't stay there. They stayed at a hotel across from Madison Square Gardens, The Belvadere Hotel. It was "Party Time Central "there was a party almost every night at that place and on the nights there wasn't, everyone was downstares in the bar. I had a single at the St. Moritz and paid $8.00 a day can you believe that. Rooms in a like hotel today would be about $280.00 Now, remember that was in 1957. I still can't believe it. I think that's what a glass of water costs now days. New York was great in those days, there was a certain energy in the air in 1957. I used to love to walk to Madison Square Gardens, past the Essex House and the little side walk restaurants like the Cafe de la Pae. It was a great feeling to be in New York in those days. I learned something about the city every time I walked to the Gardens and back. Coming back to the St. Moritz Hotel one night, I noticed that the first two letters, the 'E' and 'S' on the sign, of the ESSEX House were burned out and it said SEX HOUSE. You can bet they fixed that quick. The first year we played New York City, with me in the cast, I was given tickets for a new Broadway play called "Westside Story" I was told it was about two gangs that can't get along and get into a big fight and a couple of them were killed. I thought I can see gangs fighting in Philadelphia, Detroit or Chicago, why would I want to see a Broadway play about it. Well, that was my big New York mistake. As you probably know "Westside Story" was a major Broadway hit and became a motion picture with Natalie Wood. It won '10' Academy Awards. I missed the Broadway Show; but, I bought the movie.

We were in Montreal and the show was playing the Forum. It was an old building but it had a lot of history in it, with the Montreal Canadians and the many Stanley Cups won there. Most of the kids were staying at the St. Mary's or The Laurentin Hotel. It was such a beautiful city with horse drawn carriages parked outside the Laurencian Hotel. You could take a carriage ride almost anytime of the day or night. It was almost like being in Paris.The second year, I stayed at the Laurencian again and one morning I was having Breakfast with a skater from Paris named Christien Moreau. She said she wasn't very hungry and just wanted toast, jelly and coffee. So, being French, she ordered French toast and coffee. When the waitress arrived with her French toast. She looked at it in amazement and said what is zess!!!. The waitress said that's French toast Miss. Christien looked at the waitress and said, "This is not French toast, I am from Paris, France and I can tell you this is not French toast, this toast is "cooked". She then pointed to the next table with an order of toast on the table and said, "That is French toast." Well, as it turned out Christien wanted plain old toast. They don't call French toast, French toast in France.

Another French girl, Gigi Naboudet, a French Champion received a letter from her family, in France addressed to: Mlle. Gigi Naboudet
Ice Capades
Holy Week Lay-Off, USA

On the Ice Capades schedule the cities and dates were listed and before Easter, we rehearsed at the Broadmore Hotel and Ice Arena, in Colorado Springs, CO. It was a beautiful place. It would be snowing outside and in the mountains and we would be swimming in the outdoor pool heated and enclosed in glass. On the schedule during that weekit was listed as Holy Week Lay-Off and her Family assumed Holy Week; was a city and Lay-Off; was a state. For someone that doesn't speak English it was a natural mistake. To almost everyone's surprise, The Post Office actually delivered the letter. Do you think that would happen today.....Think again !!!

Taking in dinner and a show, on our day off. L to R, John Harris Sheridan, Christian Morreau, Gigi Naboudet Trenkler and Reg Phillips out for dinner and a show.

Ice Capet Karla Sawyer Wiley and Ice Cadet Henry Seguin back stage at shows intermission.

Waiting for their cue to go on ice.
Bobby Specht, Ronnie Robertson, Cathy Machado,
Henry Seguin, Richie Eagan.

Phil Romayn and Cathy Steele

Isn't it funny that things skaters or even old friends tell you and how you remember them….how those stories affected them and even how they affected you as time goes on and they will probably stay with you forever.. So, I'll relate a few of stories that for some reason, I'll always remember. Ice Capet Gloria Spoden was talking about the time Martin Luther King was murdered and she mentioned that armed guards escorted the cast member from the hotels to the arena and back to the hotel. It was a scary time filled with misbelief for her and many of the kids in the show and something she'll always remember. I wasn't there; but, I'll always remember her story and the fright and saddness she must have experienced. Then there was a beautiful story from Ice Cadet Nick Sherlock who was quoting the great Jimmy Durante who said, "Thanks to the people at Ice Capades, who took a little H2O froze it and turned it into something to dream about." I always thought Jimmy Durante was a comedian; but, that wasn't funny….. it was just beautiful. Then there was the story that Ice Cadet Don Lowrey likes to tell. It happened in Detroit at the Olympic Arena. There was a big curtain separating the boys and girls dressing rooms and one night, there was a tremendous bang…. And to every ones surprise, the curtains fell down, that separated the dressing rooms. Well, I guess the skaters got a show that night as well as the audience. I'm sorry to say I wasn't there….. There was another remark that was made about George Petty's girls (He drew the girls on many of the covers of the Ice Capades programs) I'll always remember it and I don't even know who said it; but, whoever it was said," When you touch the wrist of a George Petty girl, you can expect to feel a pulse." I thought that was beautiful as well. Please don't tell me Jimmy Durante said that too !!!

Freddie Trenkler, Aja Zanova and Jimmy Durante

*Peggy Flemming, Olympic and World Champion
with Ice Capet Patty Davis Gur*

This picture is of a later addition of Ice Capades, I believe in 1978. It was sent to me by Ice Capet Stephanie Perom and I believe the remark made about George Petty's girls would apply here. When you touch the wrist of one of these girls' pictured here', you can expect to feel a pulse.

Arlene Dervitz Bornstein, Maxwell Anderson, Jill Erickson Michael O'Rourke, Stephanie Perom

We took a lot of trains, they were our trains with the Ice Capades logo's on the cars (later planes) and a lot of cabs. When the train arrived at a major city in the south. I always tried to be first to the hotel. I noticed the rest rooms said "white men" and "colored men" and the same with the drinking fountains; but, I figured I'd check that out later; but, now I had to get to the hotel. I ran outside and threw my skate bag and suit case into a cab. The cab driver was trying to tell me something but I couldn't understand him. So, I just kept saying the name of the hotel. When we arrived at the hotel, the doorman opened the door and said, "Sir, white folks don't ride in Nigger cabs down here." The cab driver turned around, looked at me and said, "That's what I was tying to tell you." I felt bad about that because I was born in the north and wasn't accustomed to that, kind of talk. The cab driver gave me his card, because I had asked for it and the next day I called him and got him tickets to the Ice Capades, for him, his wife and four children. I know it didn't make up for it; but, I felt better anyway and actually saw him and his family after the show.

Ice Capades Train, Our homes away from home. I almost forgot how much fun it was on the train.

The Ice Capades Trucks. This is how we got the show, costumes, sets, trunks, dressing room equipment etc from town to town. It was Bob Recker's Department, another Pittsburgher and good friend.

This is what went on during most of the train trips but, it was always FUN. In this case it was the men's dressing room; but, only the location was different. L to R Eric Waite, unknown, Jimmy Grogan, unknown, unknown, Freddie Trenkler.

ICE CAPADES AND THE UNION

ALL OF THE CAST MEMBERS of the show were AGVA union members. AGVA is the American Guild of Variety Artists. The President of the Guild was Penny Singelton, better known as "Blondie" in the movies and on telelvision, remember "Blondie and Dagwood" ?. We rarely had union meetings when I was with the show; but, we had one in Hershey, PA and I went with my girlfriend, at the time Ginny Iverson.

The main points discussed were raises for the line (chorus) kids and extra compensation for a third show on weekends; however, I didn't pay much attention and Ginny wanted to leave early; so, we did.

The next morning I was having breakfast the Community Inn, in Hershey, PA with the ringleaders of the union meeting Barry North and Shirley Thomas. Just then John Harris walked into the restaurant. He saw me sitting with Barry and Shirley, not knowing that they were the ring leaders and said, "Johnny, I need to talk to you." So, I got up and joined him in the next booth. The waiter came and Uncle John ordered breakfast and I ordered a second breakfast. I was always hungry in those days and besides that he was paying for it. He then said, "I understand you were at the union meeting yesterday!" I told him I was and he said "Were there any trouble makers there? "That kind of shocked me a little; but, not a lot. Two things went through my mind: #1 he already knew I was at the meeting #2 He wanted to see if I was going to tell him the truth. I found myself in a very awkward situation, because I knew he had his spies and kiss asses there. These guys reported everything back to him. I knew who these guys were, because I would be in his office when they would come in and tell him things before they noticed me there or maybe they just ignored me. It would do no good to mention their names now because it would just hurt a lot of innocent people. However, some were management, two were line skaters skaters and one was a principle, a comedian. I always tried to be on the side of the kids, because I was one of them. So, I told him someone, in the back yelled out, "We want compensated for the 3rd show on Saturday's", but, they were in back of me so I don't know who said it. He said, "Would you tell me if you knew their name?" and I said, "It might be hard." he just smiled and said, "Always remember, blood is thicker than water John Harris Sheridan". Nothing else was mentioned and we just finished breakfast. I told him my girl friend said she didn't feel well, so we left early. A few months later there was another meeting and John Harris asked me if I was there. I told him I didn't go to the meetings anymore, because the kids feel uncomfortable with me being there and I respected their feelings. On top of that I couldn't repeat what I didn't know. There was never any real trouble with the union because John H. Harris and Ice Capades ran the union. But I don't think that's a surprise anymore.

I left Ice Capades after "Hans Brinker and the Silver Skater", to return to school at Phoenix College and Arizona State University; but I did work on the new show, "Carmen" with Jose Greco, the famous Flamenco dancer and choreographer. When I say I work on it, I mean I really didn't do anything creative or make a contribution to the chorography. It's just that Jose wasn't a skater and he would do an unusual step on the floor and ask me if it was possible to do it on ice. So, if I could do it on ice and it didn't look awkward, he would use the step. That's really all I did. nothing creative.

Well the show went on for the next five years, with Harris at the helm; but, health problems were starting to catch up with him and he was having marital problems at home. In 1958 Donna had left the show she said, "To take care of the children" but, deep down inside I know she still wanted to be in the show again, after all she had been doing it since she was seventeen years old. Finally, John and Donna agreed to separate and get a divorce, in 1959. John ended up in the Mercy Hospital in Pittsburgh with a severe gall bladder problem and almost died. But, Donna was there, at his side every day, with the three children. Their relationship was amicable and friendly. I think he still cared for her a great deal, especially since the children were involved. Actually, I think he still loved her. Donna couldn't stand not working so, she started to teach ice skating. at the Ice Capades Chalet, in the Los Angeles area, with her good friend and former Ice Capades skater Claudia Lattin, if not the prettiest girl, in the show she was one of them for sure. She was a good skater and a excellent teacher. Claudia and Donna got along very well and were friends for many years thereafter. Donna did very well as a teacher and had a great following, with more students than she could handle. However, a couple of Donna's new "friends" in Los Angeles ended up taking advantage of her in financial deals and John H. was always there to help her out again. And that's the way it was, until he passed away in 1969. I've always thought the world of Donna and when people told me that she wasn't my Aunt any more, I told them they were full of Crap! I still considered her a family member and I always said she and Uncle John got divorced, BUT…. I didn't divorce her; so, she's still my Aunt and to this day I feel the same way.

THE KLUGE ERA

JOHN KLUGE OF METROMEDIA, THE owners of numerous television and radio stations throughout the country, including Channel 11, KTTV-TV in Los Angeles as well as Foster-Kliser the nations largest billboard company. John Kluge got an early start in Pittsburgh, in the late 40's and early 50's with radio station WAMO a rock and roll station. It was the first station to feature a black D.J. his name was "Sir Walter Raleigh" I used to listen to Sir Walter on WAMO-Radio a small station, about 250 or 500 watts. But it kicked butt, in the town where radio began, with the 50,000 watt KDKA, the world's first radio station. WAMO caught the attention of western Pennsylvania.

After 23 years, Kluge's ownership of Ice Capades it was followed by Tom Scallen, then the The Globetrotter people, followed by Dorothy Hamill and her husband. Dorothy's husband thought he was Irving Thalberg of MGM. When Dorothy owned the show, her husband made one rule after another even eliminating the shows handling of the cast's trunks. He acted as though he owned the show himself. He started playing "Huggie Bears" with a couple of the chorus girls and when Dorothy learned about "Don Juan" and his extra curricula activities his show business days were over. Dorothy's first husband was Dean Martin's son Deano a Captain and pilot in the Air Force National Guard. He was killed in a plane crash and I don't believe Dorothy ever got over it and Dean never did either. Dorothy's second husband shared a strong resemblance to Deano and many believe that's why she married him. I will not mention his name out of respect to Dorothy. Finally Pat Robertson, of TV's "700 Club" bought into the show and within a couple of years it folded.

THE AUDIENCES STARTED TO DECLINE

AFTER SETTING RECORDS IN NEW York at Shea Stadium in 1967, that year Ice Capades played to the largest audience ever assembled for an ice show with 28,233 in attendance.

The Ice Capades audience started to decline in the middle 70's and I don't believe, as do many, it was caused, by over saturation of media coverage, that was their excuse. Naturally, there was television coverage of ice skating in the Olympics, The World Championships and The National Championships, all news worthy. However, seeing something on a regular basis doesn't breed contempt for it. If people ever got tired of dancing because it's on television too often, the Rockettes. would be waiting on table in the Bronx. So, I don't believe this happened with Ice Shows. LOOK at Disney on Ice !!!

Many times producers forget who their target audience is, for Ice Capades it was for Families, Children, Skaters and the Public IN THAT ORDER…. The most successful shows Ice Capades ever did had great family and child appeal. Shows like "Cindarella", "Snow White", "Student Prince", "Brigadoon" and "Peter Pan". Shows like "Wish You Were Here" and "Carmen" even though they were great, had nowhere near the popularity of the other shows, they missed the audience mark. What kid ever heard of "Wish You Were Here" or "Carmen"

The farther that the show departed from that time proven tradition, the more it separates itself from it's core audience. Just look at the success "Disney on Ice" is having then ask yourself, who their audience is ? "Disney On Ice" doesn't even have marquee stars. "Disney On Ice" has great skaters, star quality but not National, World or Olympic, Champions and they never promote their skaters. They have seven shows on the road and they're sold out almost every night. ….Tell me I'm wrong about Family, Children, Skaters and the Public. The people never left Ice Capades…….Ice Capades and its new Producers left the people !!!

Walt Disney with those who helped make Ice Capades famous.

I don't mean to cast guilt on former owners; but, those responsible for the shows closing, never set foot on the ice and knew very little about skating. Harris never skated; but, he owned ice rinks and hockey teams and was married to an ice skating champion. The Shipsteads and Johnson's owners of Ice Follies were also skating stars. They starred in Ice Follies for years. They knew skating and skaters. I believe that a few years after Harris sold the show, it started on it's long road to Chapter 11. Harris always returned a large percentage of the profits back into the show. But, with some of the new owners, many things were eliminated so they could pocket the profits. Trunks were "eliminated" (a very stupid move). To a performer a trunk is like a little bit of his/her home. It houses personal objects, clothes, cameras, photo albums, programs, letters, mementoes and things you can't carry in a suit case. You wouldn't believe what you could fit into a trunk, I still don't believe it, but, we got everything in our trunks.........The new owners added another performance, They invested less of the profits back into the show, costumes, music, sets, trunks promotions and even the cast suffered, because of excessive greed. The show no longer seemed as important as the bottom line. It was no longer mattered, what you put on the ice; but, what you put in your pocket........ And that's why Ice Capades died.

I'm not much of a fan, of many the owners and management of Ice Capades after Harris, because IF GREED COULD CONSTITUTE A WEAPON, THEY KILLED ICE CAPADES.

John H. Harris died in 1969, in Pittsburgh, Pennsylvania, the birthplace of Ice Capades. And after years of poor management and greed, his beloved Ice Capades died too.........

John H. Harris, R.I.P.

It was all a Harris dream which came true, from the Vaudeville Theaters, to the Nickelodeon, The first all motion picture theater in the world; Harry, Abe, Sam and Jack Warner; The Selznick's, Lewis (the father), Myron and David O. (the sons) Selznick; To the Harris Theaters; And the "Singing in the Rain" Guy Gene Kelly"; Catherine Variety Sheridan and the Variety Club; Pittsburgh's first sports arena The Duquesne Gardens; The Pittsburgh Hornets of the American Hockey League; Pittsburgh's first and only, basketball team, the short lived NBA, Pittsburgh Ironmen and finally, the world famous Ice Capades. You can be proud Pittsburgh, Look what you gave the world !!!

THE END

Every skater needs to be mentioned unfortunately I couldn't get all of their names; so, here are a very few: Jesse Quatse, Ritchie Egan, Bob Gallagher and I joined the show at the same time from Pittsburgh and we made many friends like Herb Cowman, an actor, skater, an announcer with Forgie & Larson's Badminton. June Barlow, Tiger Lilly a super talent; Mari-Jane Bodum, one of our beauties and just as nice: Evelyn Gray, our good Pittsburgh Pal and true friend: Shirley Costello, who loved Ice Capades and learned to be a line captain; Pat Matthews, was our line captain and a beauty from Australia; Claudette Marleau, our Diva from Montreal: Gloria, Glenna and Gladys Burling, triplets and everybody's friend: Marilyn Holt, one of the most considerate and best liked girls in the show; Carolyn Tingle, our Miss Massachusetts; Claudia Lattin, one of our best. I think many of the girls wanted to be like Claudia Latin; Joyce and Donna Mae Hukkala, Remember the old saying,"God help the mister that comes between me and my sister……..it's true here" unfortunately, as I was writing this section of the book I got word that Donna Mae Hukkala Barnes passed away. God must have really needed her because this time he took one of our best. Dick Eckstrom, a good man but nobody knows where he is; Ron Kenny, the show's John Barrymore; Phil Fraser, Mr. Dependable; Roberta Harris, and if I forgot to include her name, she would fly to wherever I am and kill me; Terry Hall. the shows race car driver; Mel'Mr. Lambretta' Daugherty; Lee Brink, a very good friend; Jean (John) Dauphinois, our French authority; Tom Brinker, a really good guy but another one that just vaporized after he left us; Carol Lynam, a lovely and really sweet girl; Pauline Archambeault, if you could spell her name right, you could win a trip to Montreal; Pittsburgher Billy Shea; Jack Vanderwier, one of the best; Reg Phillips, a great friend and one of my very few room mates; Joe Marshall, everyone's pal; Terry Salo, another good guy; Bob Skrak, the guy that could do everything including run the backstage coffee/sandwich stand sharpen skates and skate in a couple numbers; Pat Clohessy, a lovely and nice Pittsburgh girl; Walt Chapman, a great skater and another good guy; Bruce Wilson, another guy who just vaporized after the show and probably one of the funniest guys in the show; Betty Inghram, and if you can you believe it, another Pittsburgh lovely; Janet Knutson a very nice person and a wonderful skater; Barbara Shebatka, a beauty in Ice Capades Class in Pittsburgh and a beauty in Ice Capades on the road; Barry North, another one of the best; Ronnie Martin, a good guy, looked like a hockey player; Fred Yanke, one of the best skaters in the line; Robert Gallagher, started as a chorus boy and ended up as the company manager, way to go Bob!!!; Jack Coulter, a great skater, could have been a star, but I don't think he ever wanted to be; Eleanor White, one of the lost boys in Peter Pan; but, definitely no boy; Shelia MacFarlane and Pauline Gallagher, these girls added up to a '20' and I was lucky enough to be the partner to both of these beauties and I'll never forget them; Joan Penwarn, aka Penny she always chased the wheel in the precession number, mainly because she was the smallest girl and how could I ever forget one of my favorite girls Noreen 'Sully' Sullivan one of the very best; Robert 'Mr. History' Ricker (transportation) Patty Huber Yeates Ursetta, I'll always remember this Pittsburgher, from Sacred Heart High School; John Rodgers, my second cousin. Then there are those that came later and continued to uphold the great name of Ice Capades: Joanne Berg, Susan Carscallen, Zane Clark, Patricia'Patty' Davis Gur, Janina D'Abete, Linda Davis, Sara Dietrich, Laura Eldridge, Sue Gillham, Gitte Griebe, Mary Havnaer, Darlene Herceg, Barbara Hofstad, Nancy Kaiser, Karen LaPierre, Denise Kuchiki, Susan Auley, Lisa Marocco, Valerie McBroom, Carol McKinley, Pam Miller, Stephanie Perom, Tammy Askew, Judy Roof, Juile Savay, Sonya Shewchuk, Andrea Soma, Samantha sturrock, Mardi Tatton, Joan Wade, Ellen Wasylyk, Judy Wyspinski, Yola Young, Bev Anderson, Dean Bates, Edward Dumoulin, Tommy Fountain, Michael Fowler, John Houchen, Gary Jones, Doug Martyn, Brian Nilson, Michael Vibrany, Pat Forbes, Anthony Kudrna, Linda Devela, Gene Janouski, Jullie Elledge, Tim Estiloz, Sharon Boudreau, Dawn Rogner,

Melva Cantrell, Carolina Widom-Warner, Sonia Polson, James Gilchrist, Julie Haas, Stephan Colvin, Rozann Smith, David Hansen, Debby Cutter George, Dolena Thompson, Julie Savay Ross, Lisa Lauten Baumann, Terri DeBello, Ken 'Mr. Back Flip' Shook, Pat Golden Roman, Charlotte Vallo, Janie Broadhurst, Ginny Barker Reel, J.P. Ramano, Janet McMina Wilds, Louise Gasper, Dolena Hall, Don Lowry, Gloria 'The Blade' Spoden, Nan Horner, Nick Sherlock, Liz Taylor, Bill Bain, J.P. Romano, Michael Garren, Joey Curren, Dody Marie Baker DeMarchi, Rozann Smith, Melva Hunt, Margaret Trenkler Ramponi, Caroline Bennett and my Boston friend Corazon Ross. Again, I'm so sorry for missing so many great skaters and performers. But, even though I missed including their names, they will forever be a part of the Ice Capades Family

Ice Capades Principal Ladies Hawaii 1976: Pepe, Alison, Lisa, Sheri, Karin, and Anna.

SOME OF THE STARS FROM 1940 TO 1995

Donna Atwood	Barbara Ann Scott	RosemaryHenderson
Bobby Specht	Alan Konrad	Lois Devorshak
Janet Lynn	Helen Davidson	Bobby Maxson
Ruby Maxson	Richard Dwyer	The Old Smoothies
Freddie Trinkler	Joe Jackson	Dorothy Hammill
Phil Romayne	Terry Brent	Cathy Steele
Jackson & Lynam	Swift & Clark	Forgie & Larson
Cathy Machado	June Barlow	Herb Cowman
Sashi Kuchiki	Denise Kuchiki	Rosemary Henderson
Tai Babilonia	Dick Button	Vera Hruba Ralston
Otto Jelinek	Maria Jelinek	Aja Zanova
Jacqueline duBief	Sonya Klopfer	Jenny Baxter
Scott Hamilton	Ronnie Robertson	Jimmy Grogan
Michel Grandjean	Silvia Grandjean	Randy Gardner
Robert Paul	David Jenkins	Robin Lee
Chukie Stein	Paul Castle	Johnny Littengarver
Ludmilla Protopopov	Oleg Protopopov	Elaine Zayak
Barbara Roles	Michael Carrington	Peggy Flemming
Elizabeth Manley	Hans Muller	Hans Leiter
Margaret Field	Jimmy Lawrence	Eleanor O'Meara

Milissa Militano	Eric Waite	Guy Revell
Barbara Wagner	Arthur Clark	Judy Blumberg
Linda Carbonetto	Peter & Kitty Carruthers	
Donald Knight	Tommy Litz	Karen Magnussen
Megan Taylor	Charlie Tickner	Jayne Torville
Christopher Dean	Robin Cousins	Tiffany Chin
Michael Kirby	Jane Kirby	Toller Cranston
John Nix	Ingrid Wendl	Peter Oppegard
Lon Maxwell	Marty Maxwell	Sandy Culbertson
Willie Kall	Don Bearson	Joe Jackson Jr.
Lyall Stevenson	Lynn Finnigan	Bill Dougherty
John Curtin	Paul Castle	Chuckie Stein
Tim Wood	Orrin Markhus	Irma Thomas
Marty Maxwell	Lou Maxwell	Bernie Conboy

The Absolute END